This

is

a

True Story

by The Trailer Park Angel

ISBN -   978-1-7341109-1-3

With deep gratitude I offer appreciation to
my husband for his love,

unwavering support and belief in who I
truly am.

Also, to my therapist,

who acted as my guide throughout this
recovery and rebuild journey.

Without both of you, this story would not
have been remembered or told.

Thank you.

This is a True Story

This book is dedicated to every single victim of
this hidden epidemic;

those who cannot speak for themselves.

You are not forgotten.

Contents

This is a True Story

Preface

This is a True Story

You're here.

You've accepted the invite, turned on the light,
and looked in.

It's bright here and this level of illumination will
remain until the end.

No more dark places.

You enter now the true story of a young girl,

growing up in a small town in the 1960's, USA.

It is my story, and I've only just now put it
together.

I know that it is not a unique story and that I am
not alone.

The characters in this story are real.

Today, they are either dead, insane, hoping that
no one remembers (or talks),

or, like me, carrying on a "normal" life

with a split mind that blocked everything.

I remember now.

Tighten your seat belt.

Introduction

This is a True Story

There is no sound when a mind splits.

A natural product of terror,

the tear patiently and silently cocoons,

encasing every shred of reality within itself.

It builds then.

Layers of falsehoods bury the truth and
muffle the noise.

Secrets and lies are the stuff of whispers.

They travel on blaming fingers.

They march with indignation, well-heeled
and plump with blame.

But truth sneaks in, skinny and bare;
unnoticed.

Except for its sound.

The noise of truth is relentless.

It cannot be silenced.

Reconnecting a mind happens at high
volume.

It's loud here now, and I'm grateful for the
din.

Turn that mother-fucker up.

Welcome to my reunion,

The trailer park angel

5.13.2019

This is a True Story

Notes for the revision of 2022

The book is now re-organized for clarity. Initially, it was written following the order in which the memories were recalled. There is not really an organizing principle to the recall of trauma. It comes as it will, in the order it can be comprehended. It is almost 3 years since it was originally published, and we've lived through a Pandemic. There are several additional memories in this revision.

Some comments from readers suggested that it needs clarity. I am not surprised by this. With this revision, order is attempted, ages given to organize them, and it is hoped that in this way the story comes alive in the same way it was remembered; as 14 years of a young girl's life. Nothing has been added that is not true. Nothing has been removed that is. With the additional memories, my story becomes more of a challenge to believe. I know with every fiber of my being that what you are about to read, actually happened.

2.17.22

Read this first

This is a true story.

I'm telling it anonymously. People have died when I told it out loud the first time. That was thirty years ago.

I am proof that a deep level of depravity exists right under our noses. You will never notice it. Children will not tell you this, or give you any obvious signs. Either will the adults involved. YOU will have to watch for them and pay constant attention. To everything.

I am telling it as I remembered it. I want to convey the ability of the human mind to manage severe trauma. I am not alone. I don't possess any unique ability to withstand horror.

The torture and abuse of our children continues in secret right now because we are all so determined to survive. The will to live has no minimum age.

In order to live day to day, *the true nature of abuse becomes invisible for the victims of that abuse.* Memories are blocked and then denied if remembered at all. If they do surface, they are explained away, often by "experts", and subsequently ignored by the mainstream population. This is actually quite convenient for the perpetrators, as well as for the rest of us. It is easier to sleep at night when the most horrific nightmares are considered fantasy.

The reason for its telling now is simple. I've only just remembered it.

I am sixty years old.

But this story begins when I was much younger.

I was born in an idyllic setting; a small coastal town in the United States. I was blonde haired, blue eyed, beautiful; cherubic. It was the late 1950's. I was the third child, the second daughter. My father was an electrician. My mother stayed at home and eventually bore another daughter.

We lived in a small home on a quiet street. It was walking distance from the water.

The town was so small that pretty much everything was within walking distance. As you walked, you could stop at a local shop for a soda or just about anything, where you were sure to know the owner. I could walk to the schools I attended.

My father's parents came to the United States from Central Europe. My paternal grandmother lived just a few blocks away. I never knew my grandfather. He was found in the dead of winter, drowned. This was about 8 years before I was born. The papers didn't say suicide, but my mother did.

He was a bartender. They were very poor, there were 6 children at one point. They'd rented and been evicted from just about every house in town. My grandmother served the family duck blood soup for dinner. My father hunted and fished to help feed them. They were on welfare. Back then, when you were on welfare, they gave you shirts. My father used to say that he could look around in his class at school and know which kids were on welfare by their shirts. His mother sold herself for money. She was a tough woman.

My maternal grandparents were entirely different. They owned a farm. My grandfather was a cowboy. I used to love to go there. They lived a bit out of town and we didn't see them much. There were Texas longhorns on the walls, several barns, a few horses, a donkey and different styles of wagons. My grandfather was a bit of character. A kind man, he sold western style gear as well as southwestern jewelry. My favorite was the jewelry. He let me pick out my favorite piece, a turquoise and coral phoenix necklace. He was a jack of all trades.

My maternal grandmother was quiet. She was dignified and what I remember about her is that she always had a set of rosary beads, plenty of western novellas to read, tea to sip on, and crossword puzzles from the newspaper. She loved to garden. She cooked even when she lived alone. She was orphaned as a very young girl. She was Irish and German and very, very Catholic.

This next part comes not from memory, but from photo albums, of which there are many. My mother fervently chronicled the childhood she wanted the world to believe. It is the only one I "knew" was real, until this year.

I was always with my baby sister who was just a few years younger than I was. There were almost 10 years between myself and my older siblings. So, my life was colored with Sam. We shared a room and thousands of secrets. She was the best friend whom I adored, protected and hated in the same breath. She was the dark to my light – auburn hair and deep brown eyes. Facially and in body type we were pretty similar. Our voices were identical, and as we got older, we could fool our boyfriends &/or husbands on the phone. We had fun with that.

There was the Brownie troop, cheer-leading, field hockey. There were weekends on the family boat, swimming, catching starfish, clamming and fishing. As we got older, there was a speedboat and water skiing.

Yearly family vacations, Christmas trees and Easter bonnets. Birthdays, First Communion, Confirmation, Graduation; all of the rites of passage were documented.

These are the images that seemed to be my life. I look as if I am kind of smiling in some of them, yet I never, ever felt that I was looking at ME. It was, instead, some familiar little girl. I experienced no recognition or connection with the images of my childhood.

I was quiet. I remember loving school. As an A student, school was a place I could succeed. Once you told me what to study, I would always accomplish it, and be rewarded with an A or B. I promptly forgot it, but my grades kept me out of trouble.

At some point I became very, very chubby. Not obese, but I remember at the time, that there was a "chubby" size for girls clothing at Sears (our only local department store besides Woolworth). I hated the name, ("chubby" size), but liked how Sam and I could get matching outfits there (she wore a "chubby" size too).

Mostly we both wore hand me downs. It wasn't until I was a lot older that I realized that "hand me downs" probably weren't so cool. I used to love getting those boxes of clothing from my cousins.

Summers were spent at the beach or on the boat. My mother eventually returned to work, but she had summers off. We took swimming lessons there and swam with neighbors and cousins every day. Winters found us sledding on the surrounding hills or ice skating in the random ponds tucked in between the trees near the house. We only went home when our parents began to yell for us to come in for dinner. Each of us knew the sound of our parents hollering "Dinner!". It was a different time then, for sure.

When I was in 3rd grade my maternal grandfather had a stroke and died suddenly. This brought quiet, dignified Nana into my life on a daily basis; she moved into an attached apartment.

Things I have always retained from those first 14 years include the fact that I really loved my brother. He was sweet and often made Sam and I feel special. He was funny, skinny, and played harmless tricks on us as he got older. I never doubted that he loved me, that he loved us both. I didn't like my older sister though. She was mean.

I loved to sew and make things with wood. I loved to bake. I rode everywhere on my bike. I taught Confraternity to mentally disabled youth. I was exceptionally good at Math and won an award for it. I was terrified of my father.

I began to menstruate around the time I entered High School. My cramps were so bad that my new gynecologist prescribed codeine for me. I let everyone know how much pain I was in, and that I was now FERTILE.

Eventually I was instead put on a birth control pill, to avoid the constant taking of codeine. This was a convenient happenstance, as at the age of 15, I began a serious physical relationship with a boy who was one year older than I was. He lived walking distance from the house.

The first time we had intercourse, he remarked how it seemed odd that it was not what he expected. There seemed to be no "cherry" to pop as he put it. I remember that I barely even felt him inside of me. We were so young at the time and had no idea what any of that could have meant. We were together all the time; I was crazy in love with him.

My father didn't like him. He forbade me to see him several times. We had so many friends, Jack and I, that we got around that by scheduling dates with other guys, who'd pick me up, meet my parents, then take me to be with Jack for the night. At the end of the "date", I'd just get dropped off at the end of the driveway, and walk in the kitchen door. I used to think it odd that my parents would rather see me go out with many different guys than just one, Jack. It felt backwards, as Jack wished me no harm and was quite protective.

There are a few things NOT pictured in my mother's books, that I remember. One is that I ran away. I was about 16 years old. Jack drove me to the ferry and I took it to a Monastery. I don't know what I told the priests when I got there, but they must have immediately called my father to come get me. I was unaware of this until he walked in the priest's office late that afternoon.

He never spoke to me all the long ride back to the house.

I remember choosing a college to attend that was furthest away from my home town. I had been awarded a scholarship to one nearby, but I refused it. I wanted to be as far away from that town as I could be.

I met a boy there, Fran, and we married a year after I graduated. Jack and I had eventually outgrown each other in favor of more local partners. Fran and I had a beautiful blonde-haired son; the love of our lives. He wasn't enough to keep us together though, and we divorced after just seven years. It was friendly and we remain friends today. He is a gentle, funny and deeply loyal man.

In my late twenties, while going through the divorce with Fran, something sort of broke inside. It was then that I met Chris. He was older than I was and I very quickly attached myself to him. He seemed to be the answer to all of my pain and it took us a few years to work through our simultaneous divorces and discover what it was that we were to each other. I felt that we were "soul mates". We are still together now.

We were married a few years later. Within about a month, the flashbacks began.

I think they started then because I actually felt safe with Chris. I remember saying to him "There is something that we are supposed to do together." This was when we were first dating. You can imagine his reply.

They came as bits of stories, these early memories. Moments, carved out of entire happenings, composed the flashback like shards of glass. They stood unconnected, yet clearly belonging to the whole. They lay splintered on the floor of my mind, unable to be swept or explained away neatly.

Here's some of them...

A very young relative, (teenager), standing in the hallway of my childhood home. He was proud of his stout erection. My point of view was from my bedroom. I was tiny.

An image of a body bag. It was black. There was a white truck in which it was placed.

I see myself in a yellow dress, lying on my back, on a long table. It is shaped like a rectangle. There are men around in suits. I am two years old.

My father on his knees on the floor before me. I am sitting in a dress, in a recliner in the living room of my childhood home. I felt this this one vividly, and remember thinking that his tongue felt like a cat's tongue. I am about two years old.

I am in an infant seat, on a concrete floor that is gray. I could not yet walk. There is a killing, a dark-haired woman; a great deal of blood. This one may be connected to the body bag image.

I am in a field. It is day time and there are people outside. I feel my hands on some sort of pointy stick. There is baby, an infant, and it is on a sort of skewer. I feel the stick go through the inside, feel it pass through flesh. It is then that I see from above, looking at my body and the entire scene. I have left my body. The baby is dead.

I vividly taste an eyeball. When I remember this, I say that it is an eyeball of a goat. It tastes salty.

There is a green bottle. My older sister is using it inside of me, as some sort of rape instrument.

There is a coffin. The room is dark. The top of the coffin is shut and I am inside. It is so, so dark inside.

I don't remember any sound with the images.

I had been seeing a counselor at the time these flashbacks began. When they did, two things happened.

First, I asked for a test to be sure I wasn't out of my mind. I wanted concrete proof. She administered a test. She told me that I am not crazy, actually quite the opposite. I now have the test records to prove it.

Second, she refused to continue therapy with me. She was African American, I am Caucasian. She began to see what my history included. She feared for her life. She feared my father.

So, I was on my own. Chris and I decided to take a trip to my place of birth, to do some investigating. I wanted evidence of these things. I wanted more detail.

We got a lot of detail from the local library, and from driving around to places I was "seeing".

When we returned, my son, who was about five at the time, told me that my father had sexually molested him. My world collapsed once more.

I wrote letters to my parents and siblings telling them I would not engage with them or visit. Telling them a very small portion of what I had remembered, only mentioning the incest. I did not mention my son. I was not prepared for their reaction.

They attacked and disowned me. My mother asked me how this could have happened. My father sent me a packet of pictures from my mother's chronicle of my childhood, as well as a single rose. He told me I must have been hypnotized.

None of them asked for more detail. None of them acknowledged it as truth. They were angry and abusive in their response. I did not speak to them for ten years.

Except for Sam. We kept in touch. She came to visit. She met my children.

My godmother was killed soon after I wrote those letters. In broad daylight she was run over by a truck. I heard from Sam that my father drove to the site of the accident because he did not believe that it was an "accident". He was not close to my godmother, and this was not typical behavior for him.

I have since come to understand that she was killed as a warning to my father. To keep me quiet or else. People would be killed. People closer to him than my godmother.

I became pregnant.

Both my oldest son and I began therapy for ritual abuse.

I had several more beautiful and healthy children.

We moved and eventually stopped going to any counselors. I wanted to focus on my growing family. My son was so young. We all felt that he had gone as far as he could for the age that he was.

Ten years later, I saw them all (my family of origin) at a large family gathering that we had been invited to.

The letters were never mentioned, ever, by either my parents or my siblings. Several of my nieces and nephews, who had been told, sought me out and told me that they did not understand and did not believe it could be true. There was anger and there were tears.

Contact was scarce and on the surface. Until Sam committed suicide, about 5 years later.

Since then and until recently, contact with my family once again became a more regular part of my life. The reasons for that are varied and not relevant to this telling. Except to say that for another 15 years I continued to block the facts of my childhood. I hid them from myself, and did not mention them to anyone. Until now.

About a year ago, I was in a violent automobile accident with my children and Chris. Each day since then, I quietly appreciate that we are all still here. I will never look at life in the same way again.

This is a True Story

I believe it was the deep shock of that near fatal moment that stirred up what you will soon read. Four months later, the memories began to re-surface. This time, not only as isolated shards of glass. They show up filled in and interspersed with feeling and other faces. They fit themselves together with other, older memories. They placed themselves into storefronts, on beaches and even showed up in pictures from my mother's photo albums.

The story of my childhood is being told here, exactly as I remembered it these last few months. The flashbacks did not show up in chronological order. (Note: the 2022 revision has re-ordered them)

I want to illustrate how this happens, in a real life; in the life of an average person, you may have stood behind in line at the grocery store or the library or the bank. How absolute horror is hidden in plain sight. How the recalling of it sounds insane, *but is not.* How it is possible for deeply violent secrets to exist right under our noses. I want you to believe the stories that sound unbelievable, *so that they can stop.*

I am just like you perhaps. I have a college degree, an ex-husband, children, a home, pets, and friends. I've noticed signs of aging. I'm worried about the future of the planet and this government and for my children. I pray. I meditate sometimes. I take walks and do yoga. I attend concerts and have a smart phone and take vitamins and binge on Netflix. I love my husband and adore each of my children. I have a hair stylist, a boss and a gynecologist.

I also have a therapist and this is not because of any inherent weakness or weirdness. This is because I have known for a very long time that the deep sadness and fear I held was wrong. It was not necessary. I began this most recent therapy because I wanted to figure out how to feel, to really feel, everything that was in my life; the good, the bad, and the forgotten. What I felt most often was fear.

Well, I feel things now, and in these next chapters you'll feel them too. They are recorded and written as I saw and felt them.

There is nothing here that is not true. There are no embellishments. No attempt has been made to remove the violence and sadism that was my childhood.

This is a True Story

It will not be an easy read.

Remembering

This is a True Story

I can't sleep.

I don't know how to tell you this.

It is the screaming that is gone. Like someone removed the soundtrack from the film; a silent horror film.

If you watch survivors of horrific ritual abuse, as they tell their story – you will notice an absence of affect. I believe it's due to the lack of sound. At least, it's that way here, for me.

I'll tell you my story without a great deal of emotion. If you could see my face, you'd see few expressions. Only subtle shifts as certain words are spoken. No tears.

The full spectacle of something is never re-lived. Not completely. Not if what you are seeking is sanity. Not if you intend to survive.

There are some things I need to say. I need to say them someplace and this place suits me. It suits me now. No witnesses, save this white piece of notebook paper, this blue pen.

I hate my mother. Hate her for her weakness. For her inability to protect me. For her ignorance.

Hate her for her blaming attitude of persecution and victim-hood. Hate her for her only primary concern, which was "how would this look?"

She never protected me, stood up for me, believed me, noticed me, cared enough about me. She is worse than negligent. She is complicit. She is harmful.

This week: It was Easter on Sunday. I did not call my mother.

On Monday she called me. I did not answer.

On Monday night I wrote an email telling her to leave me alone, and that I needed time. I said I loved her.

On Tuesday I was numb. I had set my first and only boundary in my family and I did not know what to do. I spent all day looking at (you tube videos of) SRA survivors.

This is a True Story

On Wednesday, I called my counselor and asked him if he could help me with this sort of thing.

He said yes.

I cried for a long time then.

I skipped my class that night.

On Thursday, my brother called.

I don't know if she's seen the email – I don't care.

It's almost Mother's Day. (Two weeks or one week)

On Thursday I ordered flowers to send to my mother. They say "Happy Mother's Day. Love ___ and ___"

I was thinking that by doing that, I'd get her and that stupid fucking holiday out of my mind – clear my head – it didn't really work.

My brother called.

I need to go.

I need to go.

I need to go.

I need to go.

I need to go.

There are things I don't need to remember. Things I don't need to know. But I do.

I remember flesh. What it looks like. What it feels like when you put a skewer through it. It is not even. It offers resistance. It is rough.

Eyeballs taste salty.

There was blood always.

How did she not know?

How did she not know?

How did she not know?

I hate them all. Particularly my sister.

Oh my god, my sister.

She would be doing us a favor if she remained pickled.

This is a horror story.

A nightmare.

My life.

This is a True Story

I said it thirty years ago.

I lived it fifteen years before that.

No one ever asked me.

My father was a pedophile. He liked children.

They called him the butcher.

It wasn't because he worked in a grocery store.

It was because he knew how to cut up the bodies.

Memories that have been repressed don't return fully formed. They show up splintered and jagged – some parts big and close, others far away.

There is very little sound with them.

It is like viewing an odd piece of modern art. Not much of it makes sense.

What I can piece together now looks like a very sad horror story.

I WANT TO BE AWAY FROM THEM.

RID OF THE STAIN OF THEM.

I grew up in a small town.

My mother was a secretary.

My father was a technician.

I had two sisters and one brother.

I was the third child.

My baby sister was two years younger than me.

She committed suicide at age 44.

My brother is six years older than me. He is still alive, very sweet and very rich.

My other sister is eight years older than I am. She is a cold, heartless drunk who pimped me out to her friends when she was a teenager.

My uncle, also my godfather, had sex on me and with me when I was a child - age 2, 3, 4,6,8 and? (These are the dates of specific recollections, but his presence was a constant.)

My father, a pedophile, performed oral sex on me. He also pimped me out to a cult of some sort where he was known as the butcher. Also (pimped me out) to his friends. Also, to strangers.

He also sexually abused my oldest son. Twice.

This was before I remembered what had happened to me.

I will piece together my life now, and in order to do that I'll have to

EXIT THE FAMILY COMPLETELY.

I need to go. I need to go. I need to go. I need to go.

I need room. Room to see. Room to remember.

I have to see it all. So that I can <u>feel.</u>

I want to <u>feel.</u>

I want a life.

Fourteen or fifteen years.

I wish I knew how and when it ended.

I was drugged.

I was drugged.

I was drugged.

I was drugged.

I don't remember everything.

But I do see a lot of blood.

There was some sort of barn.

There was something outside.

I don't think it was a goat.

There was a concrete gray painted floor.

Why? Why? Why? Why? Why?

Why? Why? Why? Why? Why?

I think it was skewered.

I feel it.

I taste the eye.

I remember my counselor from thirty years ago, saying to me, as I was remembering something:

"How did the baby get dead?"

I left my body then (not when I was remembering, but when it happened as a child).

What I saw, is a view from above.

I keep going back there... to the house, to that house, to those memories.

Those things really happened.

Those things really happened.

Those things really happened.

Did I tell anyone? Did I tell my mom? Did I try?

I must have tried.

I must have told someone.

Who did I tell? Who did I try to tell? Who did I tell?

I told someone.

I told someone.

Remember. Remember. Remember.

What did I do? Who did I lean on? Who did I count on to save me? To help me?

Who did I trust? Did I trust anyone? Anyone at all?

It was like, it <u>feels like</u>, I protected *everyone* – Sam. My brother? Even my brother? Did I not tell him?

This is a True Story

Did I tell my mother? What about my
mother?

How could she not have known?

How? How? How? How?

I must have had <u>physical signs.</u>

I must have.

Who saw these physical sings? The doctor?

Love is not a ledger sheet

and

I am not a liability.

Love is a garden

and

I am a wildflower.

(What I know to be true)

I must have told my mother.

My mother.

When did I tell my mother?

When did I tell my mother?

When did I tell my mother?

When did I tell my mother?

When did my mother hear me?

She didn't. She never heard me.

What can I do now to heal?

What do I see?

What do I see?

What do I see?

Did I tell my mother?

I did.

I feel like I told her. Like I told her something.

I was little. She was preoccupied.

It doesn't matter what happened when I was so little...except it does.

She keeps telling me the story of wanting me home when Sam was about to be born, and regretting it.

This is a True Story

It is the same story over and over. What happened then?

The yellow dress. I see myself holding that ugly stuffed rabbit out there - my little face and that big ugly rabbit. I was 2.

It touches every part of me. Every part of my childhood.

Why did this happen?

How did I survive?

I feel dirty, disgusting, unwanted.

What does this say about me? About the man my uncle is? About my sister?

I am ashamed. On such as deep level. Ashamed.

This is why I didn't want a little girl.

What am I supposed to do with this?

How am I to understand love, in the face of this?

What do I do with this?

I feel like garbage. Who would I be able to love? To trust? To be loved by?

How do I move on?

I am closing my eyes now, in an attempt to see.

This is a True Story

It is a broom stick. I see a broom stick. Popping up. Sticking up. Behind everything else.

You must let it be there. It has to fight to emerge in your conscious brain – into this world you've   created for yourself here now.

A brown stick. Skinny. Not pointy. I don't see anything else. Just that stick. It pops up. It pops down. I see it come up.

It is a brown stick. Behind it is white. Before it is gray – not black.

Why a brown stick.

It is only a stick that I see. Only a stick that I see. Only a stick that I see.

Now red. Cloth. Red cloth wrapped around the stick. It is faint. Looks far away, like a long silk red scarf wrapped around the stick.

I feel fear. A little gulp of fear in my heart just now – my head, a piercing pain in my head right now.

The red scarf is not a scarf – not so orange-red as pink-red – like salmon, but pink. I don't know what this is but I feel anxious. Like fear is waiting just beyond the door of what I see now.

And the fear waits.

It knows it will emerge when the pink comes.

When the pink comes.

When the pink comes. It is thick. It is around the stick.

There are thoughts in my head. They are popping now, saying to me

"What is this pink that is coming?"

It does not make sense.

It reminds me, not in color but in presentation, in texture, of that swordfish steak my High School boyfriend bought for me at a restaurant once. I couldn't eat it when it came on my plate. I felt bad. It was expensive and he was so proud to take me to this nice restaurant.

But when they served me the slice of swordfish, I about barfed. It looked like a slice of human.

I never said those words to him at the time, but I thought that, and I wouldn't eat.

I digress, but that happened and I was surprised at my strong negative reaction, because I ate fish all the time.

But this looked more like flesh.

Not orange like salmon.

Fleshy. Pink.

Back to the stick.

It is not a stick.

But I don't know what it is.

I cannot see what it is.

If I go back and look now, the stick has been changed and replaced with...nothing.

Why the stick? Why the pink flesh?

I must look at this slice of pink.

I must remember.

I don't' know what that skinny stick is – it pops up and down.

There are scary things my brain is putting there now. Words with distant pictures.

These words are scary words.

I do not want to let them out.

They are beating.

They are slicing, and that one makes a sickish feeling.

It is a stripping…

Of flesh.

A beating.

I feel numb and it creeps up in my throat now.

Pulverizing, flattening to make palatable.

To make palatable.

This is for ingestion.

These words, the ones coming next – they are rushing to come out – no thought – only words…

This is a True Story

To make palatable.

Not palpable, which was the word I wanted to say.

Palatable...which means edible.

The babies are the best.

But little.

I feel funny in my head now; a feeling comes over me as I let these words out on the paper – a numbness above my right eye. And there is that feeling in my throat – it spreads to my gut.

And there are not many babies.

They take time.

Fleshy women are easy and plentiful.

Not as palatable – it takes a lot of beating in order to make it chew-able.

This is what you must do.

Soften it by beating.

Flatten it.

Get only the flesh.

There is a method of beating it.

Cut it thin, in strips.

Raw.

Does not look human.

Blonde hair – I see blonde long hair laying on the concrete – gray concrete.

She is dead and there is blood.

Now I feel the numbness come all through my body – my knees, my elbows – it waxes and wanes and moves all through me.

I don't know what I see. I think that was a beating stick.

It comes after the killing.

It is for the flesh – to pulverize it.

I don't know how she died.

It is two times.

The killing – dark.

The beating – light.

This is why I see the light behind the stick – it is outside and in a different place.

This is a True Story

A different place than the killing.

The killing was in a dark place.

I see the lady on the floor.

Killed.

Blonde hair. Blood around.

The blonde hair makes a puddle.

Why don't they drink this blood?

It is just on the floor – the gray dark cement floor.

No one drinks the lady's blood.

She is dead.

I did not know her. But they did.

Her flesh is gone now.

They ate it.

Why did they do that?

It had to be fast after the killing.

It will not last. Next day.

The eating. Many. Lots of beating flattens out the flesh.

Makes it palatable.

A big word. It means "so you can chew it. Eat it, so it doesn't look like what it is."

They beat it.

It was part of a person. Now they eat it.

Why do they do that?

They have to.

It is not to get strong. It is to stay bad.

This is a True Story

I've had a headache now, for many days in a row.

I kept seeing bloody scenes on Friday. Flashes of them, flashes of bloody scenes.

I am so lonely. So alone.

I don't know if there is a memory trying to be remembered. I am afraid of this.

I feel fractured again, and now, hated.

My head hurts.

I am cold, so, so cold. I only want to sleep now.

To close my eyes and un-see.

Un-see.

Un-see all the blood.

Heads will roll.

That's what I saw on Friday. A de-capitation. Then a body stuck in a doorway; automatic doorway that cut the body in half. It was my body.

Was it?

We were walking out of the store (on Friday). That was when I mentioned it. "I'm having flashbacks."

I feel frozen now.

I don't know what these flashbacks mean.

The blood.

One came when I was driving, too.

I am so afraid. So afraid. So afraid.

There will be no money. No place to live. No money. No one to take care of me. No place to live.

No family to love me. No one I love. No one I am connected to.

I am so afraid. I don't want to feel this, yet I must.

I must. I have to.

How will I know who I am if I won't see or feel what she has seen and felt?

What has she seen? Blood. Heads will roll.

Heads will roll. Decapitation.

This is a True Story

I am so cold. Cold. Cold. Cold.

I am so cold.

It's like I want to close my eyes, but they'll be no escape.

I want to be warm but they'll be no warmth.

Not for me. Not here. I am so cold.

I am chilled to my bones. My bones are chilled.

Exposed. It's how it feels.

Cold. Exposed.

Chilled.

The thing is, once I remembered last time, I sort of already forgot.

I sort of already put it back – I didn't feel it.

I feel fractured now.

There is a part of me holding these memories and she hides. She is the fat little girl in that picture.

She is me. A part of me who holds the floaty out – it is what keeps her afloat – so she won't drown.

I can't be afraid of the insanity. The insanity that is my life – not me. I am not insane.

I love my children with all I have – it does not seem enough.

All I have is not enough to overtake this awful thing.

The awful thing I must see.

Remember. Remember. Remember.

What awful part? Heads will roll.

There is blood now. It is dark. There is white too. White beneath the red.

White skin. Black hair.

Heads will roll.

This is my imagination. I am not sure what this is.

Is it real or is it my imagination?

There are sounds, screaming sounds.

But these are male. Heads will roll. White male. No clothes.

Screaming. Chopping.

Horror.

Lying down. It is a cleaver and he sees it coming down.

There is so much screaming.

Why can I see his face? His erection?

I don't understand. It seems the erection and the terror and the blood and the semen all intertwine.

Am I making this up?

It is too horrible to speak. How can I speak?

There is a lump in my throat now.

A lump in my throat. My body is numb.

My father accused me of having sex with a boy who came to my house once, when I was in High School. I sold bean bag frogs to match the boy's cars. The sewing machine was in my brother's bedroom, and we were in there picking out fabric.

My father accused me of having sex with that boy. I don't remember that boy. I was about 15 years old. I sewed and sold bean bag frogs. They were popular. It was a small source of income.

My mother didn't reach out to me for TEN YEARS.

What kind of a mother does that?

The kind of mother who is more afraid of what she'll find, than she is of *not* having her daughter in her life.

I am so cold.

My stomach hurts.

My head hurts.

TEN YEARS.

It is fucked up. She knew.

On some level. She knew.

What do I have to remember?

What did my mother do?

How do I reconcile my mother?

What good memories?

I never expected anything.

Remember, remember, remember,
remember, remember.

What do I see? What do I see?

My mother sends me off on a bicycle.

Here. Drink this. Now go in there.

I used to think my mother wasted money on herself, on her clothes. She told me she couldn't wear the same dress twice.

I remember thinking how vain and silly that was. I was in high school at the time. I was in high school. That is a time when you should have been at the height of vain and silly. At the height.

My parents were and are sociopaths. What I defined as love, was not.

I was collateral.

I was collateral.

What happened? What do I see? What do I see? What do I see? What do I see?

Remember. Remember. Remember.

Remember. Remember. Remember.

Let it in. Let it in.

My mother. I see her clearly now. She is a sociopath. I did not see her clearly before.

I did not see. I did not see. I did not see. I did not see.

My mother does not love me. My father did not love me. At the end of his life, he said he loved me. He said it once.

He was the butcher. He cut up the bodies. He was good at that.

My father was creepy.

He hardly said a word. It is why, I suppose, that I remember each thing he did say.

Once, right before he died, he said he loved me.

You should always tell your kids that you love them.

My goal was to raise an un-abused child.

Did I?

What is love anyway? What is love?

What are my memories of my mother?

She sends birthday cards.

She encourages me to whore myself.

She reads "dirty" books. She told me about "Fifty Shades of Gray".

It is 4:00 in the morning.

What is it I must see? What is it I must see? What is it I must see? What is it I must see?

What is it I must see? What is it I must see? What is it I must see?

What am I looking at?

I feel achy. My head hurts.

I have to let go. Stop posturing. Let go and love.

Just love.

What does that even mean?

It means to be myself, and stop *trying.*

Just be.

I don't know how to have relationship. I don't know how to release control.

I don't know how to move to the next phase of friendship, of relationship, of trust.

I don't know what to do, except to *stay away from my mother.*

My mother who sold me.

My mother who sold me.

My mother.

I must figure out what makes sense. How to act from a place of truth. Of safety.

Of self-care. Of compassion.

It means only doing what feels *pure.*

What feels real.

Who do I choose to be near to?

Who do I choose? Not because of convenience, but because of choice, of love, of care, of compassion...

Who?

I choose to see love.

I choose to see through love's eyes.

Infancy

I like lists. They keep things in order. Especially things that are not so orderly. Like rape. Like fractured minds. Like mothers who sell their daughter for money, for power, for status. I think I'll dedicate this passage to Mother's Day. My mother doesn't deserve a day. She should be shot.

They were, perhaps, the perfect couple. The butcher and the pimp.

I'm sixty years old. I am gradually getting full recall of a childhood of horrors.

I'm twenty-nine years into my second marriage. I have four children, all sons. Beautiful, kind and brilliant sons. They stand as proof of the miraculous.

I grew up in a stench; without love. Yet, despite all of that, I helped to usher in four pieces of perfection. I didn't help much, but I didn't stifle them. Somehow, because I will leave them behind me, the world became a better place because of me. I hang onto that every day.

Total recall is not all it's cracked up to be.

My first memory is of watching a woman killed; butchered??? Put into a body bag. The bag was black. I think that it was put into a white pick-up truck. (Or is that another body? Another memory?) It was dark. I was not yet walking, an infant more than a child. I was on a concrete floor – gray. It was dark. Her hair was dark brown. I was in some sort of baby seat. I began to walk at 15 months of age, so it was before that. I don't have a sense of my age.

My grandfather committed "suicide". I have the newspaper clipping. It was winter. They found him in the river. He stopped in to see my mother that afternoon. My older sister was a baby. He was a bartender. He'd lost his job and no one knew it until after they found his body.

He was probably a part of this cult. I believe that now that I remember more of my actual history. His wife, my grandmother, most likely sold herself for sex, for money. They were constantly broke. *

This is a True Story

My father used to say that they'd lived in/rented every house in town. Kicked out of them all for not paying the rent.

He grew up on welfare, my father. Back then, they gave you clothing. He said he'd look around the classroom and know who was on welfare because of their shirts. They were green or gray button shirts.

He was left back in kindergarten. He used to say that he'd flunked Kindergarten. He only spoke Polish when he started, so it seems understandable.

I don't know when he joined the cult. I imagine it was before he married my mother. I imagine it was for money, for favors.

I don't know when his mother actually bought a house. It was huge. Right on Main Street. I slept there sometimes.

Scattered memories flow in now, a constant stream of them.

I imagine she was able to get the house with the help of my father and calling in a favor. Or, maybe her second husband actually paid for it. Then he died. Then she almost lost it (the house). But my father took it over so she'd have a place to live. I don't know how they could have done that. His business was always in the red.

I heard often how he couldn't take a paycheck because there was no money. My mother was his bookkeeper.

She is another segment. A segment of this story. Perhaps one of the more horrible ones. Yet, there are so many that you may not agree. You, that nameless reader peering right now into the workings of a mind; a mind split before total recall.

I like lists. They are orderly. I'll write the memories. I'm not sure, actually I know, that this is not all of them. It is a portion. Small, yet telling.

This is a True Story

Baby   Murder and body
bag

2 years old   Town hall – many
men in suits – don't know them – driven
from my father's shop in a car I don't
recognize; blue interior, big, fancy.

2 years old   Coffin. Blood. Evil
dude. My mother and father. A sort of
baptism.

2 – 3 years old   My house. Uncle.
Shame. Wet. See his erection in the hall. My
older sister is there. It happened in my
bedroom at the time.

? Many times, & ages   Cult meetings.
Killings. Babies. Women. Sometimes Evil
Dude is there.

8 or 9 years old?   Bicycle. Me. Petal
pushers. Liquor store before it was open.
On the floor. Dirty white tile. That Italian
man who owned the pizzeria. Fat. My Uncle.
Young, twenties? Raped. Felt it. Felt him.

                    I was told to drink
this and then go in there. "There" being a
room where men were. My mother set it up.

She sometimes took the call and told me to go. Or drove me. Or I rode my bike to my father's shop and put my bike in the back of his van and then he drove me.

I see a large white house. I don't know whose house it is, but right now I think of the principal. His real name has the word "kill" in it. He was the principal. His voice sends shivers down my spine.

This is what child trafficking looked like in the 1960s. Favors. Untraceable people. Children. So many children. Men. So many. Women. Not as many, but enough.

My mother is a monster.

*March 2022: With the recall of further details and memories, I have altered this paragraph. I now suspect that my grandfather actually was a part of this cult. Two of his sons were; my father and my uncle. Another of his sons was in law enforcement in the area. It would have been quite an easy thing to orchestrate rituals and deaths with a family member on the local force. I suspect that, my grandfather may have been killed that night (there were money problems). I never heard that he was suicidal (except from my mother); quite the opposite. He drank and I've heard he was quite social and gregarious. A handsome man.

This memory was fully recalled in January of 2022, and it fills out an earlier one. I'll restate both here. Realize as you read this, that I am remembering it, and doing so with the mind of an infant version of myself. Some of my conclusions about it have been drawn from an adult mind, who has recalled a good portion of the story of my first fourteen years. In other cases, this is just a report of what I am seeing; *what infant me was seeing.* There were few sounds in the memory, and I suspect that I fell asleep at one or more points as it occurred, as it is spotty.

I am unclear why I was there. I could not yet walk or talk, and was sitting in an infant seat on some sort of table. The only family member there was my father, I think. I could feel him in the room, and knew where he was, although visually I couldn't see him. I suspect now that he either was caught off guard while babysitting me, or else it was intentionally done as a sort of grooming.

When I initially recalled this memory, it was just a snapshot. I saw several things. This first came through about thirty years ago. I felt myself in an infant seat and could see a gray concrete painted floor. There was blood everywhere and there was a dark-haired woman with big dark eyes. I knew that she was dead and that the blood was hers. That was the flashback.

Here is the full memory, as recently recalled.

I am in an infant seat on some sort of round table or raised part of the floor. It is elevated and I can see the floor below me. It is a large garage or warehouse, there are very large doors in front of me; two, I think. The floor is painted gray and looks concrete. The round table thing is gray also and sort of rises up from the floor. It's made of the same material as the floor.

I have a blanket on me. I think pale blue. I am not swaddled and not bundled in winter clothing, yet there is a blanket on me. I am not cold or hot.

At first this is all I see. I sense my father is in the room, but I don't see him. He is behind me to the right side, in the corner. I can't turn my head. I can only look the way the seat is facing. This tells me that I am very young. The room has windows in its large doors, but they are painted or something and are darkened that way.

I am drawn to look in the direction of a bright light, and realize there is another door in front of me, and to my left, that has opened. It is a normal sized door. When it opened, there was daylight coming in from a hallway. The hallway was bright, lit by sunlight coming in through windows. So, I know this occurred in the daytime.

What I see are four men. They are in suits. They are holding a chain or are cuffed, each on one arm, to a woman in the middle of them. It is like they are carrying her into the room in this way. She is spread eagle, with a chain on each limb. She has some sort of clothing on. In her mouth is something bright orange. I suspect it is a gag and I'm not sure if it is a bunched-up cloth or it is an orange. It appears very round to me.

I look at her eyes as they carry her in the room and past me. Her eyes look huge, dark and terrified. I do not hear any noise or any chanting or much of anything at this point. I do not know these men. I do not know this woman.

They walk into this large room with the woman and then turn at a right angle, walking with her to what I imagine is the back of the room, directly across from the large garage doors. This is behind me, and they have turned before reaching me, on my left side. I cannot see anything at this point. The door to the hallway has closed once they enter the room.

I hear things though. It is like splat noises. I see the blood then; it moves and enters into the space that I am facing; pools of blood on the gray concrete floor. This was just like my original flashback.

I don't know how long I was there. I don't remember leaving. I imagine now, that my father was there as "the butcher", which is mentioned at other times in this book. His job was to cut up the bodies, and package the meat. I imagine that this woman was a sacrifice of some sort. There was no actual ritual that I was witness to. I don't know how she was killed. This is the extent of what I have remembered and pieced together from this earlier flashback.

I am struck by the men wearing suits. This suggests to me that this was during working hours. At that time, people dressed differently for work. Hence the name "white collar" and "blue collar". These were "white collar" businessmen.

This is a True Story

Age 2

This is a True Story

I have remembered now. Remembered more.

I know that my uncle took me to a place. A place where the lady is. The lady with cold eyes, a nice voice that doesn't say nice things. It's a sing-song-y voice, like it is trying to be nice but the subject matter isn't, so it can't be.

It's not nice.

I am two, not three.

I see my chubby hands holding an older one.

I see my round red sneakers. I have a dress on.

The lady also has bare legs. Inside a robe. A robe that swirls. She has sneakers on and I don't think they are tied. Dirty, white, Keds.

She has dark hair. I can't really see her face, not really. Just the dark hair.

My uncle gives me to her and she takes me into a place, a room. She is supposed to teach me things. Teach me how to act.

She is a consort. She is my teacher. The one who shows me how to act with the men.

Maybe my handler. It's a job. Her job to teach me. To show me my job.

I have to wear costumes. She shows me some of them. She tells me not to cry. She tells me that if I do it this way it will hurt less. It is my job.

My job.

She uses a rope and a stick or a baton or something. She holds it against my bare bottom to show me what it will feel like.

What it will feel like when it is men.

When it is men and a penis, on me, in me.

She tells me things. Things to not do. Things to not say. Sounds.

There are only a few sounds I am allowed.

She tells me it is like a game.

She tells me about the business.

This is a True Story

She is my trainer. So that I will be ready for the men. She is my handler.

My Uncle looks to by my pimp or something like that.

I remember when Chris and I went back there, we looked things up in the local library.

There was a house I drew. I knew where it was.

In town, behind the area where the dentist was, in a section of town that I held no conscious memory of, yet I knew exactly where the house was.

It looked exactly as I had drawn it.

It was her house. Rachel something. She's dead now. She didn't own it (the house) even then, thirty years ago.

She was the lady. I knew that house, knew how to get there without a map or address. I knew because I spent so much time there.

She trained me. It was a pedophile ring.

O my god. So many pieces fit together.

Here's an attempt at a chronological order of things.

Two weeks ago, around May 15th, I remembered Rachel (or Ruth?). The name of the woman who owned the house that I had drawn and knew how to get to, thirty years ago when Chris and I made the trip to that town.

She is the black-haired lady I keep seeing in my memories. She was a school teacher, we think. Anyway, she was some sort of handler/trainer/groomer for me. She told me what to do for the men. Told me not to cry. Put things on me that felt phallic, both flaccid and hard, told me how to stand or sit or lie.

My uncle took me there, to her. He left me with her. She trained me in these things. I was young. Two or three years old. He took me to Rachel.

I first had the memory, and then remembered Rachel from the trip (the trip from thirty years ago).

Then I decided, no more talking, it was becoming too much. This just has to sink in.

It was then that I began to cry. I would hear a song and sob, I put a new photo on my phone; me at age three. I cried hard for about three days.

I canceled my class and spent the weekend with my son and his family.

When we returned, it was Memorial Day. The next day I took a walk, it took twice what it normally takes to finish the trail. Then I finished my errands for the day and started to shake. The shaking and sweating and cramping and body aches and nausea were awful.

I felt as if I was going through withdrawal, and decided that it must be that.

I'd soak through two pairs of pajamas a night. This started on May 28th, in the afternoon, and it was so severe through the following day that I began to take Tylenol and Advil alternately. Every three hours. To control the shakes.

I decided it <u>was</u> withdrawal, I could/can feel the energy move out of me when the shakes and shivers come. With the two medicines it is better and I can get some work done.

Last night was the third day, and the shiver episode was less severe. I am going into the fourth day. I am exhausted.

My counselor says it is because my brain is working like crazy even though I feel as if I am not thinking.

There is no way to estimate how long this acute phase will last.

It is four days right now.

What is this that is making me cry?

That is pushing on my brain?

I can't stop seeing or thinking about my uncle.

I keep seeing my uncle in the hallway. White shirt. Black pants. Erection. Young.

His face is young. I am seeing him from my room, looking in the hallway.

Did he live with us? My father was 18 years older than him.

I just thought of that; seem to remember hearing that (that he lived with us sometimes).

He is 6 years older than my oldest sister. She is 8 years older than I am.

Who is he in all of this? Where does he fit in all of this?

How does he fit?

Was he a part of the cult?

There are no consistent images. Only him in the hallway. White dress shirt and black pants like a Chippendale dancer.

I don't know why I said that. Why he sought me out at my father's funeral.

I have to stop now.

Why did they do that to me? Why did they
do that to me? Why did they do that to me?
Why did they do that to me? Why did they
do that to me?

I am not crazy. This has really happened. As
I gave pictures to my son for his recovery,
he made it real. His cousin was/is 5 years
older. Five years older than he is. It is real.

This happened. I know this is a dream. Yet
as much as life is real, this happened to me.

I was taken by my father. My mother did
nothing to protect me.

She has never done so. Not in this life. Why
do I feel I must protect her? Why are we not
allowed to say things?

What I want to do, to say is, to expose it all
once again. To exit the matrix.

I'm out of here.

I want to leave the matrix.

What would happen if I did?

I would not be conflicted. I could see these
memories full. No fear of retribution. No
conflict.

I could see these memories without conflict.

How can I see what they did to me and then go there?

Go to that town?

How can I see?

I am beginning to hate her, hate the family. It is the family I chose. I chose this family. Chose to pack in lessons and lessons and lessons.

Why?

(A little later the same day... I drew I very tiny stick figure.)

This is me.

See how little I am.

I am very little. If you didn't know, I am abused.

I am raped. I am little. They put things on me, in me. They put things in my hands. My little hands.

My little hands.

You see, I want to wear nice things that are pretty.

I want to wear nice dresses, but I don't. Dresses show your legs and when your legs show, bad things happen.

They reach in your dress with snakes and bad things happen. They hurt. The snakes hurt.

The hands hurt.

It is better if I am not little. This is what I think, but then – the bad things happen anyway.

The bad things happen. They happen.

They happen in petal pushers. In red sneakers. In white sneakers. The bad things keep happening. If you are little when they happen, it is confusing.

(I drew a picture here. There is a table and I am lying on the table, at the end. I am so, so little. I have a dress on. It is yellow. There are 4 stick figures around the end of the table where I am lying. I wrote "These are the scary men in business suits – brown. 4 men.)

It is a sunny day.

It is in a room at the town hall, but in the back.

It is the Oddfellows sign on that building.

I don't know what they do.

I think it is the scary snakes again.

I am so little. The table is so big. The men are standing around.

But it hurts now. I write that but I don't know what hurts. Something comes out of me then. The snakes, and it is messy and I hurt and feel wet down there.

When you are little, they hurt you, because they can.

You can get big and then maybe they will stop hurting you.

When you are big, they grab you more. They push you.

It is like they hate you.

I feel big and bruised now.

Pushed around.

It all piles up on me now.

This is how it feels. Things piling up.

Bills, work, chores, family coming, phone
calls to make, exercises to do.

What piles up now all feels like work.

It is hard to act.

I want to sit here now and be safe.

(Here I drew another very tiny stick figure.)

It hurts when you are little.

It is the blood they go crazy for in the
robes.

Then, not in the robes, they go crazy for the
white stuff. The white juice.

It is not nice.

Not nice here.

Not nice here as a human. This body is little at first and it keeps getting put places. Places that hurt, places that are uncomfortable in arms that don't hold me nice. That don't hold me with kindness.

I am a specimen. A thing. A thing that became beautiful and this was treasured. It held magic power over the big men.

They were not supposed to hurt me. They were not supposed to be doing this. It was frowned on - not allowed.

I was to be saved for the king or the prince. But they couldn't wait and they wanted me to themselves. For themselves.

It is because of the snakes. The snakes are hungry. They want to feed them.

They are careful to clean up after themselves so there are no bad blood marks on the table.

It is wet anyway. The snakes are messy eaters. It is me they want.

It is wet anyway, and just yucky.

It hurts so much when the snake eats.

The men in brown suits are in the sun. They stand in the sun and smile at each other and they all tuck in their snakes, put their snakes away.

I had to wear a dress because it was fancy. The men in the sun had suits on, so no one could see their snakes.

They tuck them away.

I don't know what the snakes eat, but it hurts me.

I don't like it when the snakes come out.

I don't like it when they hurt me. They tell me it is me. That I have magic power over the snakes – they listen to me and save their hunger for me – that I command them – I command the snakes.

The snakes have to stay hidden. No one can know about them. It would be bad if people knew about the snakes.

This is why it is secret. I must not cry.

The one closest to me holds my mouth. So, no one hears.

The other one holds me down so I don't move. I cannot move when the snakes come.

If I move, the snakes could die.

It is our secret. I am bad. I have to control the snakes. It is my job to control the snakes, to keep them under control.

This is because of who I am.

This is a weird planet. Sick and weird. It does not feel like love. It does not feel like home.

No one here cares for me. No one here knows me.

But I know them. I know who they are.

I didn't want to be with them. I didn't want this lifetime. I tried to stop it each time.

But in the end, it was the only way.

The only way to learn. I am an impatient god.

Now, this many years later, I wonder if I will ever know love.

I only imagine it now.

This is a True Story

Yesterday my mother answered the email.

I am sick inside. My gut hurts. I've just poured a cup of coffee that I cannot drink.

I am freaking out with anxiety.

Later that day I received a text from my brother. I deleted it.

The habit, the programming is so strong, so powerful a pull – that I cannot even see it – if I am going to do this. If I am going to heal.

I was drugged.

I see myself as a little girl, taking a small cup and drinking it. I was injected also.

The drug is the same drug that they give/gave the sacrificial virgins so they wouldn't fight.

The doctor & his wife were both part of the coven, the cult. He had roses lining the walk to his front office door. Right on Main Street.

I want to remember it all.

I have such a headache. Yesterday, I had one pretty much all day.

A headache. Sometimes my left ear hurts.

The anxiety feels like pain in my chest.

I want to remember everything. Everything.

I want to remember the sex part. What was that?

As I write, a chill runs through my entire body and I become so, so cold.

So cold.

I want to remember the sex part.

The memories I have are not connected; the liquor store, the bedroom, the living room, the town hall...

Now I remember a coffin.

I remember being in a coffin and I see red. Red robes are what I think.

Black and red. Are the walls red or are there candles in red glass or something around me - me in the coffin.

This is a True Story

They put things in there with me. White things.

I am little.

Are they flowers or am I hallucinating?

What do they put in there?

They are standing around me in red robes, putting things in with me and on me.

These are some things I've remembered.

A coffin. I am little, less than 2 years old.

I have a dress on. It is plaid or patterned somehow with black, red, green and yellow lines with like a white bib in the front and there is white on my sleeves, on my little arms.

There is red around me. Red.

It is like liquid.

They put me in liquid. Blood or tinted liquid, but it is red and it is on me.

I am in it. I am put in it, laying in it.

It is in the coffin.

It is dark.

There is darkness around the coffin and people. People in red robes around the coffin.

They carry me, carry my body. More than one of them pick me up.

I am laying straight now, flat-like, as they carry me.

They are chanting.

Many are there, beyond the ones who carry me and lay me in the coffin.

Many others are in the audience.

The chanting goes on. There is a word with "M". A word that sounds like CHRYSTO or CHRYST. There is a word with an "L".

Is it Latin?

I don't recognize the words, don't recognize the language.

It is dark though.

Maybe red candles or red globes around the candles.

I am so little.

I am in the head of the coffin, the top end, at the front of the coffin.

Directly in the middle/center (at the foot of the coffin) stands the scary man. He wears black.

He is old. So old. A scary man.

I've seen him in other memories.

I believe he lives in a city on the East Coast.

He is very old and not fully human.

On his right, which is my left looking down from the top/head of the coffin, is my father.

He is young. He wears a robe and the color changes in my head now. It is green or purple, it does not appear to be red like the others.

He stands to the right of the very scary man. He stands to the right.

They throw, drop these flowers on me, white flowers.

But I think that happens after the coffin is closed. It is closed.

With me in it.

The chanting stops. It is quiet.

I am supposed to be quiet. It is silent.

This is a True Story

Some sort of noise comes and the coffin is opened.

I see my mother then.

She stands to the left of the scary old man.

She wears purple, I think.

I am lifted out.

There is excited chanting now.

I am undressed. Naked.

I am supposed to keep my arms up. Straight up. They wipe off the blood.

The white gown goes on me then, eventually, but not for long.

It is not a fancy gown. It is like a covering, over my stained, messy body.

I stand with my arms up.

My mother was there.

She is a part of the coven.

Of the cult.

The other thing I remember is roses.

Roses lining the walkway to the doctor's office and home.

Roses were/are a sign of that coven.

I realize now that I've sent my mother 36 roses for Mother's Day.

A fitting farewell.

I will change the card.

<u>I AM DONE.</u>

*Collateral: *Something pledged as security for repayment of a loan – to be forfeited in the event of a default*

My mother was there. My mother. My mother was there. My mother.

My mother was there. My mother. Watching. Approving. Standing. At the foot of a coffin. A coffin filled with blood. And her daughter. Her 2-year-old daughter. Me.

Me.

In a coffin. With red. Surrounded in red. It's all I see. And the people. The red people. Throwing white things on me.

Lifting me up. Up and out. After the dark comes the white things. Then I'm out. Up, over the side, and out.

They take my clothes off then because I'm messy. I have to put my arms up. I have to put them up. Up and out a little, like a V – I see now it's like a V. I didn't know it was a V then.

I was too little.

Too little.

I was too little. Like a V. My arms up. So little.

My mother was there. It is all a lie. All of it is a lie.

My life. The one I thought was mine.

The one I thought I lived.

It was all a lie. All a lie. All a lie. All a lie.

I was not loved. Not ever.

I was a piece of meat. Used.

Collateral*

Why would I say that? Why would I say collateral? I don't know.

I went to my father's funeral. It was like burying a king. They shut down the streets.

My mother was part of it. Part of it all. How could she?

The only way is if she didn't love me.

My mother was there. How fucking dare she wonder why Sam killed herself? Killed herself.

Her daughter. My mother. The spineless, weak, energy vampire that gave me willingly as a sexual sacrifice to a cult.

My mother. Gave me to a cult.

Then, pretended to love me for the world.

She was 29 years old. Old enough to realize what she was doing. I was her third child.

Her third. Did she give them to the cult too?

What was my life like, really? What was my life like, really?

Is it safe now, to see? Am I safe?

I thought I was safe. Safe with Chris.

Safe here now.

Safe to see.

My head hurts. My eyes are so heavy. So heavy. They hurt.

I will write my life. Maybe, as I do, pieces will fit together.

I keep thinking of opening lines. Opening lines for the book, the book that comes from a diary. A memoir. A life.

A life that is still being lived.

My life.

Start here:

I didn't want to be born. I know that, because of the miscarriages.

Words have no filters and so can't help but tell the truth – mis-carriage. These three prior attempts to carry me into this life were missed. I stopped them.

Me. The angel with silver/blue wings the size of Texas stopped them.

I did not stop the fourth attempt and thus was born.

On a hot summer's day in 1958 I was born. Born to the butcher and his pet, his puppet, his spineless, lizard-wife. Both of them greedy, eager and ready to devour me.

Remember what I said about words. They can't help but tell the truth.

Memories that are re-covered look very different from those that are re-membered.

Re-membered memories stand together in a straight line the first time – right out there in the light of day. They show themselves together. One continuous story, re-membered for another telling, clear and linear and easily followed. Each time the same.

Memories re-covered come from a darker place. They peek out and show themselves in fragments, with sharp jagged edges that don't fit together. Not like a puzzle, but like broken glass. Even pieced together, there are cracks and awkward connections.

This re-covering shows them, yet still vaguely.

As if beneath a film; a veil of confusion still arguing with itself.

This re-covering happens in fits and starts. Each time reaching for another piece. Trying it here, seeing if this is where it fits.

In the midst of all this membering and covering there comes a sense of gratitude.

Grateful to at last have some sort of memory. Fractured and gaping as it is, *it is all mine.*

All this talk is fair warning.

My story is not easily told and will not be easily understood by you. Yet it is all mine, and in its telling becomes part of the glue holding me together – sixty years later.

You are asked nothing more than to hear it.

First there was the word. Words can't help but reveal truth. Within these words my life is revealed, and thus made real.

I've wanted to title this "River Dead – tales of the Butcher" for reasons obvious to me and anyone who knows me. Other titles include "Santa and the Lizard." "Daughter of Santa Claus" "Born to a Cult" "Trailer Park Angel".

None seemed perfect. A title will emerge with the telling I suspect.

So, I'll begin...

(Perhaps this is the real beginning...)

It is a fact that I was born, this time, on an island. My childhood home stood at the head of a river. There was a movie theater, a small Sears department store, two banks, a town doctor with roses lining the walkway to his front door. His wife was also his nurse. He was just about a block up Main Street from the funeral home. He and the funeral director were friends.

Across the street from both ran the river, the backdrop to town. A town of farmers and merchants with one hospital and no McDonald's. Not then anyway. It was 1958.

Some of the farms had horses. Many had ducks. Most grew potatoes.

There was a small Jewish temple and two large Catholic Churches. One had a mass in Polish and other in Latin. Both had Elementary Schools attached to them. I attended one of them.

I don't know if the members of the Satanic Cult came from both churches or just the one my family attended. The reason I don't now has to do with the contrasting way in which the services at each are re-called.

Going to church happened in the light of day. I re-member what I wore, where we parked, where we sat and who else I saw sitting there. It is clear and it makes sense.

I re-covered my attendance at the cult rituals and it is still dark. The heads are cloaked. It's fuzzy. I feel confused and drugged. There are few sounds (in the re-covering). But none of these negate these rituals; they merely color them.

There's been a month of memories. Right now, I sit here, on the green couch in my new sky-blue sweats, with teeth not brushed and hair not combed, feeling a mess. A real mess.

I just realized something. It is that my childhood home is no longer a home. It is that I must make THIS my home. This my home. At least for now. I have no desire to be home-<u>less.</u> I guess I am in shock.

She was there.

My mother was there.

My mother, the witch.

My mother, the self-serving, self-centered, self-absorbed, inhuman, bitch of a woman.

This is my mother.

My mother sold me to a satanic cult. My mother sold me to a satanic cult. My mother sold me to a satanic cult. My mother sold me to a satanic cult.

She stood there, in a robe, to the right of the evil dude and she watched as they dressed me, lowered me into a casket of blood, threw white things (flowers?) on me, chanting and then covered me; put the top on the coffin.

It was silent then.

They. Were. Silent.

Then they lift the cover. And the sound changes.

My father is to the other side.

Red all around, but my parents are not in red. They are in green.

Green? Or purple?

In the middle is the evil dude. He wears black. His robe is black.

I am so little. So frightened.

When they look over (the sides of the coffin in which I am), I see red. The hoods. It must

be the hoods. It is the hoods I am seeing.
The red hoods. I think that's what it is.

It's over now. I am pulled out. My arms go
up. I am up. Covered in sticky stuff. It is
yucky. I am naked. The ladies clean me. I
was naked.

My mother let them put my naked two-year-
old body into a coffin of blood. She stood
proud near a reptile who was evil incarnate.
I can't see his face due to the hood. Old.
Evil.

My mother.

Sold me to a satanic cult.

I am afraid of losing my mind. What else?
What else? When else can I see her? What
else did she do?

Fucking cunt of a woman with no power, no
backbone, no love. Oh my god this is my
mother.

My fucking mother.

I AM NOT A DEFICIT.

My fucking mother. When else was she there? When else was she there?

Remember. Remember. Remember. Remember. Remember.

Remember. Remember. Remember. Remember. Remember

Remember. Remember. Remember. Remember. Remember

When do I see her? My mother, the bitch. My mother, the witch. She does not get a by. She does not get a by. She will see this. She will deal. Her world, let it fall apart. Fuck motherhood and my duty as a daughter to thank her, honor her.

Fuck motherhood. She is evil and greedy and it's all about her. She plans to take money from me once she's dead.

ONCE SHE'S DEAD.

This is a True Story

Age 3

I've had three days without withdrawal symptoms. I spent those three days moving one of my children into their new apartment.

Upon my return, I began again to have withdrawal symptoms; shaking, chills, feverish.

I had been thinking about what my childhood was really like. About who my parents really were and what it was to grow up in such a family. It is all becoming very real.

I am taking over-the-counter medicine so that I can function, work, drive. Down time is not as long. I am exhausted though.

I sleep pretty much all night now, until the meds wear off. This is far better than it was at the beginning, and the duration seems shorter.

I suppose that with acceptance there will be these conditions, and I'm taking it to be a good sign. That it means acceptance is happening.

Today I tried an experiment.

I have a photo of myself at three years of age. I am alone, in an Easter hat and dress coat. I look so miserable, yet I am forcing a smile.

I went into a meditative state to speak to myself from that moment. This is what happened:

I did reach her, (three-year-old me). I asked her why she was so sad, why her eyes were so, so sad. I crouched in front of her.

She said that she hates pretending but she knows she has to.

I asked her why she has to pretend?

She said it is because of her father. He will be mad and upset with her and there will be more "man stuff" for her to do.

She said she has to do the "man stuff" and she doesn't like it. It hurts her bottom.

She knows she is good at it and does what the "mans" say. Sometimes she stands. Sometimes she sits. It is naked man stuff and she doesn't like it.

Her mother gives her to the "mans" too. Everyone knows this is what she is there for.

It is her job.

I told her that I wanted her to know that she was valuable all by herself, without the "man stuff". I asked her if I could hug her and she let me, but remained stiff and did not hug back.

I got the impression that she retained some sense of self-worth because she knew the "mans", as she put it, liked her.

Also, that her father, somehow, she knew that her father perceived himself as important because of what she did. I did not get a sense that she knew he was paid for her services, only that his status was somehow tied to what she did.

It was enlightening and heartbreaking to see and feel her.

Some thoughts are coming up now, about me. At three. It feels important to note them so I will   just relate them here. They occur as a result of contacting myself (telepathically) yesterday.

First, it was a shock. The first shock was the sheer force of her. She is/was a fully formed person. She held no concept of herself as "little" or "lesser than". She realized she was small, but dealt with it.

Next, she has a sense of worth and although it was/is clearly missing key elements necessary for emotional health, it was intact and all hers. She had no judgment.

This realization has an impact for the care and recovery of young children who have been through this sort of abuse.

She knows what's happening and in her own words will tell you, without shame. Seemingly without feelings.

Things she said to me during this conversation include:

"It's my job"

"I'm good at it, that's why I have to do it."

"It's my job."

She commands respect. She does not see herself as wrong or doing anything "bad". She has done what she has, in order to survive.

Period.

She is not happy. Yet also doesn't see happiness as necessary or even as an option. She is keeping herself safe. She will not tell anyone about what has happened/is happening because if she does, she'll die. She knows this.

She is highly attuned to her intuition and keyed specially to fear. She knows why her parents use her, what she is to them, and has gotten a sense of value from that. She has worth (because of this idea of value that she developed).

She is not going to trust you for a long time, if ever. There is no benefit to trust and she does not know love or care or protection.

She allowed me to hug her (during the telepathic conversation) and in that moment we made contact. But she didn't give an inch.

What I want to get down on paper is this – Children living through this kind of abuse are surviving because they've made decisions. These are not wrong decisions and to tell them so, will do nothing to help them. Any sort of recovery from this on an emotional level will only happen with full acceptance and an absence of fear.

They are fully formed human beings in horrible circumstances and very little bodies. Yet they are powerful. They are strong. Their will to live is extraordinary and their clarity crystal clear. Do not underestimate them or question what they say or do around this. They know.

They need trust and acceptance and at this point in my own journey, I'm not sure what else.

I'll talk to her again.

My head aches.

What I keep thinking about is me, at age 3, making the decision, all of those decisions. I was so young. I feel myself there now and my/her determination. It was the only thing she could do.

It was the only thing she could do.

I had to either accept the role or die. That's how I saw it.

I saw myself alone. Alone. There was no love. There was no form of protection. I participated and cooperated as a form of/a way of protection. I wouldn't die if I did what was asked.

I knew death was an option. I'd seen death before I could walk.

My parents gave me to this cult. My parents gave me to this pedophile ring.

They held no remorse or doubt or idea of <u>not</u> doing that.

My father did not receive Holy Communion. He told me, when I asked him, that it was because he had stood up/ (been a groomsman) at his brother's wedding, which was Protestant. That was bullshit.

I even asked a nun at the Catholic High School I attended at the time. "No" she said. "The Catholic Church has no such rule."

My father benefited in many ways from selling me.

He used to brag about always having things done "on a handshake".

My parents were monsters.

Although, she is still alive, so a more accurate way to say it is "My mother IS a monster."

My mother.

I never felt protected or special or cherished or loved.

My brother was nice to me, yet not protective. He is a kind person, yet I always felt he was clueless as to what was really going on.

This is a True Story

Why do I have a headache now???

I'm fully clothed under the covers with a heating pad and shivering.

What is it I am trying to see?

What am I trying to reconcile?

I decided who I was at a very, very young age. I counted on no one. I saw no one had the power to protect me - no one with power at all.

My father, the butcher, was using me so he could get prestige and other things - land, loans, positions, things he could not afford.

His power came from me.

From my "job" as I saw it. Not real power.

I was afraid of my father.

I was afraid of my father.

I try to remember my childhood and my actual real feelings about my parents...

My father - fear, judgment, slimy, dark, dangerous.

My mother – surface, greedy, shallow, preoccupied.

I don't recall love. It is as if I've been crying all night. That's how I feel right now; exhausted and spent of emotion.

I didn't sleep well. On and off with chills and sweats all night.

What does this mean???

Who was my uncle in all of this?

I can't stop looking at the Rachel Chandler stuff. The images. The children. The smiling children.

The one especially. The little girl, can't be more than two or three – holding a knife over another little girl who lies with arms and legs out on a Pentagram.

A Pentagram.

Painted on the floor. Blood. Painted there too.

Then the photo of the line-up – in robes – to a red door.

Black robes. A red door. Dark.

All of those skinny children. Solemn faces.

I always hated having my picture taken.

Always.

The photographer at my wedding to Fran, asked me to remove my shirt. I refused.

I never told anyone. Maybe Fran, I'm not sure.

It is all so sick and tied to my town. My family. My childhood. My life.

I can't stop seeing the Pentagram. The little girl.

At first, when I first saw the picture, I didn't see the knife. I actually didn't see the knife.

That is just wrong. Somehow my brain blocked it out.

I knew the picture felt sick, but I didn't see the knife.

I was a little girl too.

I was a little girl too.

All I see is black. I'm blocking big time.

I was a little girl too.

Something about a blindfold.

I'll stop now.

(Later this same morning…)

Dirt floor, Pentagram, dug into dirt, candles, robes.

I am little. On my knees, next to head and arm of what must be a child, not much bigger than me.

I am two or three-ish, stabbing over and over, not holding tight so I don't feel it cut through the flesh, the insides, the way I did once, (but that was outside and I saw it from above, that was a spike/pointy end).

This was a knife or blade but the handle was long, it went over my shoulder, my right shoulder. I keep turning my head to the left, squinting my eyes so I can't see.

Turning so far, I don't hear anything.

Stabbing at an angle to miss the heart, the heart is important.

Surrounded by robes, black, and candles.

Dissection.

I am lifted, still kneeling, changed to a dress, a blue dress.

The old man is behind me when I am holding the knife.

He is not surrounding me, like the others.

Dissection – heart – I keep cupping my hand, it is how I hold the heart.

I am kneeling before the old man, hold my arm out with the heart in it.

The others are lined up to either side of him.

He does not take the heart, someone to the right of me does.

I am lifted away now, taken away.

I think of women doing this, lifting me away after the dissection and the giving of the heart.

Do they eat the heart?

Does the old man eat the heart?

He is old, skinny, powerful because of magic, dark.

It is dark there. I think it is a barn.

He is not the evilest. There is someone he answers to, but these people are afraid of him.

He is also afraid, somehow, I know this.

I think it was a boy. Where do these children come from? Who is Ruth?

Why does Rachel Chandler not go out of my head? Her photographs? The blindfold?

That is enough for now.

A memory.

I am young, less than four years old.
Around 3 years old actually, tiny. I have a
dress on. I am wearing red sneakers. I am
drugged.

I am standing in front of a being. This being
wears pointy black shoes, dress pants, long
brown/rust colored coat. It has a suit on
with a tie. The tie is green with an image on
it. It is a wide tie, wide at the bottom.

The image that is woven or painted on the
tie is of a dragon or a lizard. There are dark
green to black scales on it, with a long tail
behind it.

This being is not human. It wears a fedora.
There is no hair. It has taut brown skin and
strange sideways teardrop eyes. It has a
weird nose; I can see the nostril. Its skin is
smooth.

It has gloves on and it sort of guides me
into the room, after reaching over me to
open the door.

It is very bright in this room; very bright. It
is open in the middle. There is a circle. It is

a basement. The circle is outlined by people. They are robed. Dark red with hoods. Men and women. Every so often there is a reptile being – a sentinel. It is green, this sentinel. It wears some kind of vest with red on it. There are six of them, I think. They are standing upright in the circle, within the circle of people.

The feeling is expectant. The being (the being who escorted me into the room) is dressed well, as am I with my dress on and red sneakers.

It is like a bullfight. I am in the middle of the circle now and they let a being, another brownish reptile being, in the circle with me. It is larger than me.

I see it held down on its back by the sentinels. I see its penis. It (the penis) is very long and skinny and sort of pops out – straight. There seems to be something dangling from it, from the end of it – skin? I am not sure what that is. A hook of some sort? It is the same brownish taut skin color of the being. There are scales on its belly.

I am placed on its body and on its penis, (which is erect, not flaccid). The sentinels are holding it down and holding me on the penis.

The being is beheaded.

I see myself holding a bloody knife, yet I know I would not have had the strength to behead this being.

This reminds me of those animals (spiders?) who mate and then bite off the head of the male once they've mated. It is some sort of similar ritual.

I recognize none of the faces at this point. I am not "there" emotionally for this memory. I am seeing it from a distance. I may have left my body. I am seeing it as if it is a dream. I know there is more to remember, yet I can't see it yet. *

*This appears to be yet another way in which I was sold as a child. Neither of my parents are in this memory. I am certain I was drugged.

This is a True Story

Age 5

This is a True Story

There is more detail now. I am about five and Sam is about three years old. We are in the back of a car, with my uncle at the wheel.

It is nighttime and dark. I am on the right side. Sam is on the left. We are driving west, heading back to our home.

(Somehow, I know this, feel where everything is. There was basically one road going east/west through the town and I can feel our direction by landmarks I recognize.)

Sam is quiet, not saying anything, looking out the window and at me. She seems to fall asleep.

She has a dress on; white socks. Little black shiny shoes with a strap.

I am not sure what I am wearing. I keep looking at her.

Now I see us together in a brightly lit place. The floor looks white. I see us together and imagine myself with my arms around her protectively.

There are people around us, but not close. Circling us, but sort of in the shadows. It is so vague that I believe we were drugged. I think I was holding her hand at one point.

I think/feel/remember that this was an attempted initiation for Sam. It didn't go well. She didn't cooperate, wouldn't do what they asked/told her to do.

I am inwardly so proud of her for refusing.

There are few clear sequential memories here. I don't remember what else took place or what specifically was attempted. I only have a sense she refused.

I remember returning to the house. My uncle laid Sam on the bed in our room and left to go to the kitchen. I hear murmuring and I don't know who he is talking to.

She still has her shiny shoes on and I take them off of her. She rolls over to big Joe (her very large teddy bear) and stays sleeping.

I don't remember anything else about that right now.

I must have gone to sleep myself then, as we shared a room. I don't remember.

That is all I recall for now.

This is a True Story

I've had a back ache for the last 3 days.

Three nights ago, I woke up from a dream. There was a doctor. He had to cut off these large lumps on my back.

One night ago, I woke with a dream of being covered in blood. My torso was covered in blood. It wouldn't come off.

This morning, I woke up with a song in my head: "Here's to the ones who didn't make it back home."

My head hurts now.

My back seems to have stopped hurting. I think it stopped because of some more detail I recalled yesterday.

I sat down for a bit and tried to focus on the image of the back from my first dream.

It wasn't my back that I was seeing, but a back, a man's back; large man, broad shoulders and tapering down. Fit. A light seems to be shining on it. It is shiny. It is dark around it, like this takes place in a dark room or something. Broad shoulders. Shiny skin. Taut skin.

The back is bare and it is all that I see. I don't see a head or arms even.

It seems to be draped over something, something roundish. A wide pole maybe or a barrel. It is dark brown.

The scene I am seeing looks like this: (picture)

It's like all that I can focus on is the back. It looks huge to me. I can't make out any head or arms or even legs - only this back. A man's back.

I don't know how old I am. I see my father as a younger man. I see my mother as a younger woman. The two women are chatting. It is very casual.

My father has to make cuts in the back. The back is dead. The cuts are like strips. Strips of meat is the word that I think of. From top shoulder and down to bottom. It is a large back. It is a muscular, white skinned back.

It is all so very casual. I see white butcher paper.

This is a True Story

It's like my father is butchering the carcass for people. Wrapping it up for people. Like any other piece of meat.

Only it is human. It is human. It is a man.

The man is dead.

My father is butchering the man.

The man is dead.

It is that people are waiting for the meat. You have to butcher it while it is fresh.

This seems to be a scene from my life. It explains my brother and the ketchup scene.

This was a part of my life. It was what my father did.

My father the butcher.

This is something I saw more than once, more than as part of a ritual. It is so casual. It seems to be just a common occurrence. I am just there. Watching my father cut the back into strips. They are packaged then.

I see it and I have now written it, yet it sounds unbelievable. But it's true. It's what I see.

I believe the back is so large to me because I am small, and it is the focus of the memory. A bright light shines on the back. I don't recognize this place. Like a warehouse or something. It feels like a large, vacant room or garage or empty warehouse.

It is where people come to get their meat. Their human meat.

Cannibalism.

That seems to be what this means. As I write the word, my back hurts again. I suspect I am remembering yet another part of this gruesome upbringing that was mine. I know these things, feel, sense, and see these things now. These scenes I had locked away.

These scenes I forgot.

These scenes from my childhood.

Not like the pictures in my mother's photo albums.

These images are real. Flesh and blood. Lots of blood.

My father the butcher.

I have to stop now. This is enough. This is enough.

Age 6

This is a True Story

For as long as I could remember, whenever I visited my paternal grandmother's home, and ventured upstairs, I'd be struck by a sort of vision/memory. It always felt weird. This was a memory of me, sleeping in a twin bed and looking out the window, noticing the shadows of the cars passing by (she lived on the Main Street of town). They were showing through the shade, which was pulled down.

The room had two twin beds. The bed that I was in, stood horizontal to the window and on the other side of the room. The other bed, was placed vertically from it, with its edge against the wall that held the window.

There was a string with a glow-in-the-dark traffic light hanging from the overhead light in the middle of the room. The beds were metal, painted light green, I think. There were braided rugs in the middle of the crowded room, covering a linoleum floor.

The thing was, I could not consciously bring up the memory of anything else about sleeping over there. I did not know if I slept there often, or why. It was a scene I'd return to check on, often, while visiting my grandmother as a child. It was as if, in retrospect, I wanted to check to see if those things were really there, the window shade with its wavy and fringed bottom, the glow-in-the-dark pull chord, that metal bed, the braided rug, the tissue box with the fancy pastel colored design cover over it.

I've since recalled the reason for my frequent return to that upstairs bedroom. Here's what I now recall.

Of note, is that I have not wanted to see this. As evidence, it's been 2 years since I've had any additional memories (It is January 2022). I have felt that there was something further I needed to see and it was hampering my ability to function. I was constantly shaking and frigid, as if the very blood running through me had been refrigerated. I was, once more, sweating through my clothing when I slept. It was inconvenient, to say the least.

I went into a meditative state and began a process that has been successful before. I began to focus on whatever showed up. The only thing that did, was my uncle. At first, I could see nothing else. Then, I had a little angel show up in my vision. It was me at about 3 or 4 years of age. She/I was standing in front of me with her little hands on her hips, saying "I'll show you, come on". She was wearing a gray and white dress and sneakers on bare legs.

So, I took her hand and found myself at my childhood home, in the front yard. We walked around to the back yard and proceeded along a path I also knew well, through the woods behind the houses on this dead-end street. The dirt on the path was sandy, this was an island after all. The trees were not thick and sunlight shone through the leaves on them. I was unsure where we could possibly be headed, and as I thought that, she showed me a house. It was a big white house. The further we walked; the destination became clear. This was my paternal grandmother's house. It could be accessed without much trouble through the woods behind my childhood home.

It was large, with a huge enclosed front porch. My grandmother grew indoor plants in that porch. I used to love the violets. There were so many.

We went around the back of the house to the kitchen door. This was up a concrete staircase, and had many locks on it. Somehow the door opened and we were inside. It was just as I remembered it. She was hurrying me through the kitchen and wanted me to go upstairs. I didn't want to. She again said "You have to, this is where it is".

We went to the top the stairs and I felt a bit like a giant; the ceilings were so low. We walked around to the front bedroom, which was in the NW corner of the house. She walked all the way in, stood against the wall and looked rather satisfied with herself. She said "It's here". Then, she just sort of stood there, watching me.

This was the room I had re-visited so often in my childhood. I stood there for a bit and surveyed the room. Everything was there. My baby sister showed up, in the bed against the window, sleeping under the covers. It was summer. I could see her light night gown with blue-green little flowers on it. I guessed she was 3 or 4.

Next, I found myself in the other bed, the one that was horizontal to the front window. I was about 6 years old. I was lying in that bed, but I was not asleep. Then, I heard my uncle, who also lived in that house, come into the room. He would have been about 20. I suspect it was summer and he was home from college.

He pulled the covers back and my underpants off. I had been holding the covers over me and now was lying on my back. He wore a t-shirt and I think boxer shorts. He was sweaty and smelled unpleasant. I suspect, now, that what I smelled was alcohol and sweat. I have no idea what time this was. He raped me. As he did, I turned my head and looked out the window, watching the cars go by and casting shadows through the pulled shade.

When he was done, he grunted and left. I felt between my legs, it was so wet there now, and it hurt. I was so afraid and ashamed. There would be wet marks on the sheets; stuff was leaking from me. I sort of cupped my hands there and made my way to the tissue box with the fancy cover. I grabbed tissues to wipe myself off, and as quickly as I could, wiped off the sheets. I stuffed the tissues into my over-night bag. It was a zippered thing and was brightly colored. I didn't want my grandmother to find these wet tissues. I found my underpants and put them back on, climbed back into bed, pulled the sheet over myself, and eventually fell asleep.

This was one of the tawdrier recollections. It tells me that my uncle, who is also my godfather, used me for sex whenever and wherever he desired. He seems to have been a sort of handler for me in other memories. I don't frankly know how often this happened. Yet my attempt to quickly cover up the "evidence" indicates that it was a familiar event. The thing that stayed with me is the deep shame I felt. I was six.

Age 7

This is a True Story

Another memory.

I'd been thinking about ... "how did it happen?"

"How did I get removed from my home in the middle of things?"

I'm putting pieces together and this is one piece I don't have. I had remembered returning home, but not specifically leaving home.

Mostly (in my consciously remembered childhood) I was with Sam, so I wondered how that all played out.

I decided to try to remember without writing it down. I closed my eyes and focused.

I immediately see Sam and I in the family room, sitting on the floor. There is a hassock between us and our Barbie dolls are all around us. We are in the midst of playing. I feel like I am about seven years old. And she is about five. I'm wearing a striped t-shirt and pants.

This is a True Story

I see my father come in to the doorway to the room. He wears work shoes, a green short sleeve button shirt and dark-ish brown pants. This means he's home from work. It is early in the day so it must be a Wednesday or a Saturday.

I hear him say "It's time to go Spook". "Spook" was his sort of term of endearment for me, if you could call it that. I didn't look at him.

I looked at Sam, our eyes met but no words were exchanged. I had a doll in each hand, I put them down on the hassock and got up.

I walked back to my bedroom and put my shoes on. They were tan with laces.

I walked into the kitchen and followed my father out the kitchen door.

I don't see my older siblings around. I see my mother hanging clothes on the clothesline in the backyard, as we get in the jeep. It is tan and old.

It seems like a long drive. It is to a house set back on a cliff of some sort above the water. I think the Sound. But I am not 100%

sure of that. It is big. As we pull in, and this is the only thing I remember my father saying to me that day, he says "You know what to do."

A dark-haired lady comes out and walks to the car. I get out and she takes my hand and walks me to the house. My father never gets out of the jeep. He pulls away.

We walk into a huge foyer. It is ornate and there is a winding staircase. The dark-haired lady I have seen before. I know her.

She takes a small plastic cup of pale, blue, clear liquid and hands it to me. I drink it and give her back the cup.

We walk through a doorway to a room. There are clothes hanging there. I am a bit confused as I remember this, because I see two things... One is a plain, white frock – no sleeves and just below my knees. The other is a fancy little girls dress. Light blue, puffy sleeves, about knee length. In any case I have sandals to put on and they are brown.

I hear the dark-haired lady say, "I want you to look pretty."

This is a True Story

We walk down a hallway to another room. The walls are wooden, like a library. Low lighting. I don't know if the room is round or what but in front of me is a semi-circle of men, all well-dressed. About five or seven or nine of them; more than five but not ten. It is dark and I am short so I don't see their faces.

The dark-haired lady moves behind me to my left and sits in a chair.

Things are getting very fuzzy here and I suspect it is the blue liquid I was given.

I go in front of the first man to my right. I don't remember what happens, only that my bottom is exposed, I have no underpants on, and I am passed from man to man.

The last man is close to the dark-haired lady, and she takes me out of the room. I am very groggy and lie down.

When I wake up, I am back in my clothes, my own clothes, and I walk out of the house with the dark-haired lady.

My father is there in the jeep.

I don't remember any conversation. When we pull in the driveway, the sun is lower in the sky and there is more activity. My older siblings are home. My mother is in the kitchen and it feels like dinner is being prepared.

I don't remember anything else.

This is a True Story

I'm just going to write.

It is sunny. The parakeets are going nuts, squawking is what it sounds like.

My hand is so tired. I guess I am so tired.

I had a muffin. I am drinking coffee.

My hand is tired. I am thinking about my trip back to where I was born.

There seems no end, no end to these memories. I know one is here, here in my mind.

It waits now to emerge. It waits... This memory.

I was cute. I was not always over-weight. No, not always. I began small.

I was small.

I was small.

Why did they do that to me? Why did they hurt me so much?

Why did he? He – my father? I remember calling him dad. Sort of, but not. Not really feeling the dad thing. The dad vibe.

I didn't get it, never understood it.

We didn't dance to daddy's little girl. I don't remember doing that. It got left out. Left out of the wedding.

My wedding.

What tries to come up now? What is waking me up? Knocking on my brain? On my head?

What is it?

This pen is hard to write with.

I am angry today. Angry and scared. Scared silent.

Now that's a phrase, "scared silent".

In my mind's eye, I don't see anything. Nothing. Black.

Scared Silent. My home town.

Where is a herd of purple unicorns when you need them?

They are hiding too. Are they Scared Silent?

I don't know, but I imagine them without voices, but with big eyes.

All of this always feels made up. Until I feel it viscerally. It becomes part of me then.

Part of me, of who I remember myself being, feeling.

It cannot be made up then, not fake.

I feel it then.

It is because of Sam. I am so freaked out because of Sam. I am about to return to that house, that house where it all happened. Sam was there.

Sam may be there again. She may be. It's not certain, but she may be. She may be.

She may be.

She calls me back there whoever she is. She calls me back to that house. That house where it all happened.

The beatings... What?

The beatings. They happened there.

What beatings? I remember no such beatings.

Only once I remember. She was grown. We were older. Teenagers.

She sneaked out of our bedroom window and walked in the freaking living room door. It was 2 AM and he was there. It was the beating then. For her, a beating.

I remember thinking that I didn't get one, didn't get a beating, because I got all the other stuff.

He wasn't supposed to hurt me or leave any marks.

That memory pops up now. The one with Sam. Her huge brown eyes looking at me.

It is light brown paneling, either the floor or near her, near her face.

I don't know how little she is, but not too little, not a baby; a girl.

I am big.

Not two or four but seven or eight or nine. I feel big.

I don't know where we are or even see what is happening. But I look at her and say with my eyes "This will never happen to you. I'm doing this, it is happening to me, it won't happen to you."

I tell her with my eyes that I'll protect her. I think I am seven. I see how little and scared she is, she wears red or I see red.

It is near to Christmas. I know what's happening. It is red near to Christmas.

I don't see anything, but I feel like I am standing.

I am thinking it is the living room. The brown is from the paneling.

The Christmas stockings.

She is standing near them. The light shines off of those shelves or the mantle or something there. She stands near the mantle.

I only see her and red. It must be the Christmas stockings.

It is like she has to watch.

I feel as if I am naked. Naked and standing up.

But I don't know where I am exactly or who else is there.

I can see that she is afraid.

My big mind wants to make sense of this, this image of my scared baby sister.

But my little mind is focused on her.

On her eyes. On (me) being big and brave so she won't have to be.

I'll do this. I'll do it every time so she won't have to.

But she'll have to watch. I can't help that or stop that. She'll have to watch always.

He makes her.

She hates him. I hate him too, but somehow, I know he won't damage me physically, won't hit me.

I cooperate.

I feel these things. My body naked or mostly naked. My pants are not on my legs. I am standing up. I have full view of my sister while something happens. It happens down there.

Down there in between my legs. It is where I go to the bathroom. That is the big exciting place. The place he wants in.

This is a True Story

He, he, he, he, he.

I keep wanting to put my father in the picture but I do not see my father. I feel something happening, something happening down there.

I do this so she won't have to. I protect her. My baby sister.

He won't hurt her, but she has to watch.

I don't cry out. I must be big and brave so she knows I will protect her.

My baby sister. Nothing like this will happen to her.

Nothing like this.

Later the same day there were more details about this. They came at 2 in the morning, so technically it was the next day.

It was winter. Snow out the window.

Man's shoe. Brown - old fashioned dress shoe.

Black pants tied with a brown belt; worn, older, with a silver buckle.

Skinny. I see pants crunched up inside the belt.

Tan shirt. Pattern, with white, check or plaid. Different collar. Tan, but ridged or something, not buttoned down.

Brown hair, darkish.

Young man - teenager? Don't recognize or know him; green eyes.

Sam in the corner against the mantle, big eyes.

I am standing up.

I don't feel anything, but he is kneeling down. I don't know what he is doing.

I don't feel or remember anything else.

This is a True Story

I desire intimacy. Closeness. Trust. To feel love. I desire to feel love.

My head feels weird...

What is supposed to happen? I will sit for a moment...

I feel anticipation, fear, threat...

I keep seeing paczkis.

Something changed.

I was seeing lots of paczkis. Then, the paczkis I was seeing began to wiggle as if they were alive.

What I see are tiny legs wiggling and arms wiggling.

I see a long pole.

I keep seeing wiggly legs - naked baby legs - longer? I don't know if they are longer but now the legs seem longer; still naked, still wiggly.

Somehow, I know that there are throw away women - women birthers - killed eventually - I think of that woman Sam told me about.

I see dark hair - baby hair. Not a boy.

I am very afraid to keep seeing these things.

There are no children now. There are only parts of wiggling bodies - wiggling, trying to get away?

Scared - screaming and screaming and slashed.

Masks of monsters to scare them. Little, very little wiggly legs held up in front of others - other screaming things, other wiggly things...until parts come off and splat noises came then.

It seems there is a point where the screaming stops. That is when the kill is completed.

The terror has maxed out.

It is then that the splat is heard.

There were eyes, robes...I don't know why I had to watch. I sat aside now, I don't know if I was physically aside or I'd left my body.

I'm older here, 7+ years?

Cups - hoods. Squeezing, slashing.

This is a True Story

Dark around the edges, light in the middle.

The birthers were irrelevant – never saw – strays...

I don't know why I saw this.

It looks now like a grooming process.

His (my father's) business was sold for only 25,000.00. My mother was a secretary. How did he afford the boats, the property, the loans to his brothers? The take-over of his mother's mortgage? How come the offer of the paid wedding ring from his "friend"? The offer to pay for graduate school if I moved back home?

I want to remember so that I can feel...I don't see anything right now. It is so fragmented.

Age 8

This is a True Story

I've recalled another memory.

I've had highly anxious feelings. These cause chest pain, as well as headaches.

I've had them for several days now.

It all feels connected to my uncle.

My uncle.

At first, I recalled him at my father's funeral.

Fat. Old. Smiley.

Then I saw something. In my mind, I saw something that made no sense.

It was a boy. Maybe ten or eleven years old.

Skinny. Naked. With arms up on either side of his head.

Although, I don't see his face. I don't know if that is because I'm blocking his face, or that his head is pointed down, or his head is gone.

He is dead.

The way that I see him is with his arms shackled to a tree. I see green.

This is a True Story

I don't see his feet; just his body and legs, hanging.

Like this: (Another picture)

He has white skin. But at first, I also see darker marks around his abdomen. I see this from a distance.

I am going to say here what I saw, what I "know", and what I heard.

I am about seven or eight years old.

I know that this skinny boy, the one now shackled to the board and on the tree, was struck with a sort of whip. I see him being lifted to be mounted on the tree.

I don't know if he has his head.

He is young. There is no body hair.

It is daytime.

This is outside.

I am now in front of this boy's body.

My father is to my left, sort of even with the tree but I can see him so he is forward from the tree.

To my right, and a way back, is a young, mentally retarded man. He is in anguish. He brought the boy to the group.

They tricked him.

I don't recall how the boy is killed. I've kept it blocked.

What I see is me, standing in front of the boy's body.

Behind me are five or seven young men. They are younger than my father is. Directly behind me is my uncle, who would at this point be in his early twenties.

I see a blonde man and a curly haired man to my left on one side, and a slick, greasy haired man who I think is a politician, as well as a dark-haired man to my right and behind me.

It looks like this: (Another picture)

Obviously, this is not to scale. (Meaning the picture that I drew)

What I sense is great building excitement.

I see grinning, smiling.

Especially from the greasy man.

There is an arrogant machismo to this group.

There are no robes.

I don't know where we are.

There is not chanting, but yelling. They are yelling.

"Get it up."

"Keep it up."

I am supposed to put the dead boy's penis in my mouth.

I am supposed to do this until the signal words.

I do not see what they are doing, but I think it is known as a "circle jerk".

I don't know what the words are to make it stop.

It is awful and I've blocked it.

My father is there to take down and take care of/dispose of the body/the boy.

I don't recall much else, only that they yell louder and louder and seem to be getting off on seeing me put the boy's penis in my mouth.

I don't know who killed the boy. He was so skinny. So young.

The retarded young man is devastated throughout this. It was meant as a sort of message for him. To keep him in line. So that he would obey them.

He brought that boy to them.

My uncle is a sick, arrogant prick. I am reminded of the rape on the beach. I wonder if it was the same group of men – only that many years later?

Sick, sick, sick, sick, sick, sick, sick.

"Gonna need some whiskey glasses, if I'm gonna see the truth."

Not a rooster, but instead this country song sings me awake this morning. Tells me where to look. Look through the glass, the glass that holds the liquor.

The glass of the liquor store window.

Look at the floor beyond the glass.

The white tiled floor. The one that was dirty.

The one that held my face and my body, my eight-year-old body in pedal pushers that were light tan.

It wasn't open yet, but Tracy let me in.

I rode my bike, not to the store but to the shop. My father's shop. It was around the corner. Around the corner from the liquor store that wasn't yet a liquor store. They must have been building it. I know what the inside looks like without shelves or counter or anything. I knew where it was. I'd been there before. It was across the street from the tavern.

This was a particularly brutal rape. The owner of the tavern was a big man - huge actually - obese. He hurt me. The floor was hard and my face was pushed into it. I was face down.

There were three men there. My real uncle who was 14 years older than I was. My fake "uncle". I don't know why we had to call him uncle. There is no family relationship.

Two or three of them raped me on that floor. I especially remember my uncle, remember what it felt like. I remember thinking it felt like a snake was inside me.

I was drugged.

Pretty sure about that. Don't remember after.

I don't know what it is about these pedophile rings, how it is kept a secret. Do they think that the children won't remember?

I almost didn't. Almost didn't remember.

It is the fracturing. And the drugs.

And the pictures...so many pictures. My mother's pictures. Showing her perfect life in books that are numbered. Filled with hundreds of pictures, some black and white.

But you see pictures can lie and they don't need photo shop.

And glasses that are tinted with rose colored blood and whiskey? They eventually see 20-20.

My childhood is coming in crystal clear.

I am drinking my tea. I woke up with my children on my mind. Then worries, money worries. Charges I don't recognize or understand. My tea is Plantation Mint. It has CBD honey in it.

I have a huge headache. My nose is runny. I took Oscillo*.

My kitten is sleeping on me now. I have tea, a heating pad, my kitten, a humidifier, CBD, Acetaminophen, the heat is on, a sweatshirt, a quilt on me and I'm on this beautiful couch. I'm not doing this alone. I am safe.

My kitten is yawning.

I am safe. I am safe. I am safe. I am safe. I am safe. I am safe. I am safe. I am safe.

No one can hurt me now. I cannot hurt anyone now. It is safe.

I am safe.

What they don't know is that they put tools and knives in your hands; in the hands of children. Very little children. They put tools and knives in your hands. So, you feel it.

You feel it going in. You feel it coming out.

This is a True Story

There was a faint flash of light to my right just now, near the humidifier.

There was another one, to my right but further back.

My head hurts.

This tea is good. Not too hot but warm and very yummy. It is almost gone.

My kitten is cleaning himself. He must feel safe by me here now. It is weird. I can't imagine anything feeling good near me right now.

I'd like to stay here and curl up and be warm and safe and unexposed. Here now I am unexposed. No one is asking me to do anything or be anything.

No one puts a dagger in my hands and tells me to push. No one.

There is no force here. No one in charge but me. I am in charge. I am safe and I am in charge.

It's a new world. Sometimes I feel as if time is disappearing. Like the day slips on through and time is immaterial to it.

Sometimes I feel that Chris goes places in the day and is disconnected from time. Me too.

I feel disconnected mostly, except when I am in the schools. Then I am very time oriented.

I digress now.

The cat has settled in to sleep. It feels nice to have him here. If he did this every day, I would like him more.

They put a knife in your hands and you are little. It is more of a dagger.
Silver/gold/bronze with hints of black – ornate. Or is my mind now filling in that part?

It is a dagger (I drew a long, pointed dagger with a wide handle here), like that. I see it in front of my eyes.

A dagger.

This is a True Story

They put it in your hands and make you hold it to carve. There are carvings to be done. Not whittling like on a tree trunk. No. Not whittling. Not any sort of trunk at all.

Not a tree. Not a trunk. A dagger.

They put a dagger in your hands. It is silver and has designs on it. It has a point. The point does the carving.

Not a tree. Not whittling. Carving.

I can't see anything. No people.

A dagger. They put a dagger in your hands. It is bigger than your hands, but it is the point that you need. The point that you use. The point that carves. It is the point.

What is carved?

I can't see anything.

I can't see any people. I only see the dagger. They put the dagger in your hands.

The dagger.

The point is what they use, what you use. It is like an instrument. A tool for carving.

What is carved? It is not a tree. Not a trunk.

It screams.

All sorts of images come into my mind now. Eyes. Eyes. Eyes.

No eyes. No seeing. Take eyes out.

The screaming. I can't hear it, but it is so loud.

The X's for eyes. The eyes are gone. They are gone.

I don't see any people around, but they are. I know it.

THIS NEXT PART IS PRINTED AND QUITE LARGE. IT REFERS TO MY FIRST RECALL OF MY HISTORY, WHICH TOOK PLACE WHEN I WAS THIRTY YEARS OF AGE AND INCLUDED SEVERAL MEMORIES OF RITUALS AND OTHER ABUSE.

AT A CERTAIN POINT BACK THEN, I DECIDED I HAD REMEMBERED ENOUGH. THAT I HAD A LIFE TO LIVE AND A CHILD

TO RAISE, AND I WILLED MYSELF TO STOP
REMEMBERING. I STOPPED ANY SORT OF
THERAPY. THERE WERE NO FURTHER
MEMORIES UNTIL NOW, THIRTY YEARS
LATER.

I remember thirty years ago tasting an eye.
Having an eye inside my mouth.

I was not little, not tiny, not two or three,
but older. Eight maybe. I was eight. It tastes
salty. Eyes are salty.

I don't see this, but feel it, know it, taste it.

I don't think I can do this anymore, but I'm
not done.

I had thought (when I was thirty and
recalled this memory) that it was a goat.
What is a goat?

I am confused.

Memories, knowings, tastings, feelings are
scattered and disconnected and jumbled.

They put a dagger in your hands and you
have to do it. You have to do it or they
skewer you. Like a spike – they put you on a
spike and watch you die. They save your

blood then. It is worth more if there is screaming.

They are greedy, hungry for it. It is hideous, yet I am so frightened I don't look at their faces.

They crave the blood, want the blood, drink the blood.

It drops off of their faces. They gorge themselves.

They put a dagger in your hands and you have to use it. You have to use it so the blood is on your hands AND NOT ON THEIRS.

BUT IT IS NOT BY CHOICE. NOT MY CHOICE.

IT IS: DO THIS OR BE SKEWERED; OR THE NEXT ONE SKEWERED IS YOU.

IS ME.

They put a dagger in my hands.

I cut out eyes.

How did I do that?

How is this real?

I can't do this anymore...

Later that same day...

I just read this.

My face hurts. My head hurts.

When I read this, I did not cry.

I am going to read it again. First, I'll take some Ibuprofen.

I first looked at some childhood photos of me.

I know why my mother keeps talking all the time.

It is so there is no room for the truth to creep in. Random and constant thoughts are a great diversion; a constant obsession.

WOW.

I am going to read it aloud this time.

I am going to see if I feel it.

This is a True Story

A memory; I am 7 or 8 years old.

I see a similar, maybe precisely the same scene that I've seen/remembered prior to today. It was a few years ago now; there were parts of babies, they were being dismembered.

I see a light, a brilliant, huge and living pulsing light – white and yellowish. It is surrounded in deep blackness – it is huge. Is it a ship?

It's to my left. To my right is where I am seeing/witnessing the dismembering of the babies.

I look at the light and then see that there is a room of sorts, and there are beings in there. I only see the silhouettes, so they are black shapes walking around in stark contrast to the brilliant light. I imagine that there are rectangular metal tables, tables where they are preparing the babies. It is like a plant.

These are skinny, angular beings with big heads. They look robot-like. Very far away.

Then I see stairs leading up to where these beings are. They (the beings) come up and down the stairs to get the babies and children and parts, body parts.

Then there is a female being. She is very tall with robes on. She seems to be smiling, but her mouth is so small. HUGE eyes. They are oval, but come to a sort of a point on the outside. Huge gold-blue-green eyes. She wants me to go with her. She's reaching out with her hand. It is long, three fingers and knobby, white-ish. The skin on her face is light green. There are scales. No hair. Large head.

She is much taller, or seems to be much taller, than the black silhouette beings. They are short and numerous.

I don't want to go with her up those steps. I think "whoever goes up there doesn't come out".

The next scene is this huge creature. Huge. He is located in the place where the silhouette beings are located. He sits back with his huge legs spread. He is in a chair. It is a throne. That is what it is. There is light all around him. He's in the same light and place/area/ship/room/portal as the silhouette beings. The silhouette beings scurry around him. They are to my left, while looking directly at this ship/portal/light, and he is to my right.

I come up only to below his knee-cap. He is naked. His skin is deep purple, so deep as to be black. He is huge. His legs are like tree trunks. He has dark claws on his feet and hands. He has horns.

There are spikey points around his shoulders and I believe down his back, but I do not see that. Not from where I am standing. He has the spikes and horns on the top of his head like a crown would be, encircling the top. He has a snout. His eyes are close together and small, relative to the size of his head. His eyes are above his snout. It (the snout) sticks out from his head. He is drooling. He has a large phallus and it hangs between his legs. He wants me to stroke his phallus.

That is all I remember. *

*After this memory I did some searching online for a deity I'd heard of – BAAL.
I see many images of BAAL and another deity – MOLOCH. Some of them are very similar to the being, the huge dark one, that I remembered. None are exact.
In reading about MOLOCH, I see that he is mentioned in the Old Testament as a deity who demanded child sacrifices.

I never put much credence in the Bible or the Old Testament, thinking it to be mostly made up of metaphors. Having seen this creature and the dismembering of the children, I think that what I witnessed may have been some sort of sacrificial ritual. It took place in what felt like some sort of star-gate or portal. There was an other-worldly sense to what I witnessed. I have no precise way to describe or define it.

The memories are a bit fragmented, though connected. I suspect that I did participate somehow, yet I have not recalled the details. I was clearly drugged for this; the memories were not out of body memories though. They came from within me and I felt real fear, if subdued, as they were recalled.

What I did not record in the retelling above was that my father was there. He is off in the distance. He is young. He is talking to some men. The men are older than he is, and there is a feeling of subservience that I get from him as I observe the scene. Clearly, he brought me there at their bidding. I suspect, now, that he was paid for this. He looks nervous. He is not near me, but I see him. He is to the right of the stairs and the huge dark deity. He is not on the ship/portal. He is on the ground, the place where I was at first. He is not in the light, but in a sort of shadow from it.

He watches. He does not come
close to me.

This is a True Story

Age 9

This is a True Story

I don't see anything. It is more of what I feel.

I have a headache. I am cold. So cold.

I woke up so many times last night. So many times.

I have chills. I have a headache. My head hurts.

I am frightened. I have chills.

I painted my fingernails blue. They are in such bad shape. Such bad shape.

My body seems to be not in very good shape.

I am reading that book now, so that I can help myself to heal.

I feel so cold. So cold.

I am angry. Becoming angry.

How can I do this? How can I go through all of this? How will I come out on the other end of horror? Of pain?

My head hurts in waves now. I sense a numbness. It moves through my body. It brings heat with it. I want to take off my robe. It has become too hot.

I will. Hold on. I will.

Now I have chills again. I took some Oscci*. It should help.

Now I don't know what to write. I don't know what to say.

I keep seeing the photo of the two little girls. The pentagram.

The knife/dagger thing she holds.

They have such beautiful faces. They are so tiny. So small.

The one holding the dagger is smiling. I can't remember about the one lying on the floor.

Rachel Chandler, child handler.

Where do they get these children? Where do the children come from?

Rachel Chandler. Rachel Chandler.

Skinny. Desolate eyes. Supposedly models.

Not models. No. Victims.

These children are victims. No one chooses horror. No one picks manipulation.

There is masochism, yes. But from where does that spring? Is that a purely sexual connotation?

No one chooses to be on the receiving end of abuse for a life-time, or even part of a life-time. Not consciously. Not for pleasure. Not on purpose.

Sex is supposed to be chosen. Sex is supposed to happen on purpose.

I didn't know why the first time I had sex with Jack that it didn't hurt. I didn't know why I barely felt it.

I don't know how to talk about sex. How to feel about it. I am afraid of it.

I have memories of being raped. In them there are pictures. Scattered images.

A floor. A towel. Me, little. Me, on a table. Me, ashamed.

I don't know how sex can be beautiful. How it can be good for you.

I used to love sex.

It was a thrill.

Now (that I remember) it feels shameful.

Did I ever feel like a little girl? What am I doing right now? Is this a memory? Is there a memory trying to come out?

What is it that is waking me up at night?

Why am I so angry?

My mother. I just thought of my mother. How it would be, <u>IT IS</u>, easier if she forgets me. If I am not in her life reminding her of what she did to me. Of what she essentially gave permission for – of what she <u>ALLOWED</u>.

I stopped for a minute. Something has stopped me.

I don't yet see.

The heat is on. I have a deep chill.

Last night I kept waking up either cold or sweating – either cold or hot. Cold or hot.

What is it that I won't see? What am I blocking?

I see me, at about nine or ten years of age, on the floor of the liquor store. It is white. The floor is dirty.

Right now, I experience a sharp pain in my right hip.

I want to connect to my body – connect to ME. FEEL.

I want to feel things. I want to trust.

I want to be consistent. I want to know what trust is. What love is.

I am writing very small now and close together. My writing has changed. Why has my writing changed?

I am feeling fear. I am feeling afraid. Afraid. Afraid.

Please don't hurt me. It hurts so much. It hurts so much. I can't write any smaller now or it will be disappeared.

I want to be that small. I would like to disappear. So, they can't find me.

So, I can't be found.

They are so, so scary and mean and there is no safe place here. No place where I can rest.

No place where I can be. No one I can trust. No one who will keep me safe.

No one who will hold me and keep me safe.

I have to make myself small. I have to make my words small so no one can see them or hear them or discover me. I am so afraid.

I feel my arms around my knees. I feel my eyes big – I am hiding my head so I don't see.

Why? Why?

When will this part be over?

There is no one for me.

There is no one who will hold me.

No one who will comfort me.

No one I trust.

No one I look in the eyes to see.

I see my brother. I imagine him kind. I imagine feeling as if I know he doesn't know how much I hurt.

Yet, I know he will comfort me. I know he loves me.

He wants to make me happy. Make me laugh.

Right now, there is a deep pain going through my head. It goes from my throat up to my head, through and upwards to the tip of my head. It comes and goes and leaves a residual pain – I want to choke.

I feel there are memories. Painful, awful happenings that I can't see. Won't allow myself to see.

My head hurts so much as I say/write this. It is sharp. It comes and goes.

I am little.

I want to make myself littler. I want to be gone. To make myself disappear.

I don't want to hurt anymore. I want to be loved.

I am so afraid.

I need help with this.

Pre-teen

This is a True Story

I woke up about 1:00 AM, I was very sweaty.

I feel as if something is looming. Is that the correct word? Something is sort of knocking on my door. On my consciousness. Something wants to be seen. Something.

It has to do with my uncle. With my godfather. I've been crying lately.

Little things make me cry. A song, an image. I seem to cry easily. I keep seeing my little self.

I keep thinking about my uncle.

He played such a prominent part in all of this. He's still alive.

My uncle.

Fourteen years older than I am.

I need to see. See this thing I'm afraid of. This think that feels connected to my uncle.

Why is it so hard now?

Why are my ears ringing?

What is keeping me awake tonight?

What woke me up?

What is in my head now, is the beach. The stories my friend was told about me. Told about me when I was thirteen. Eighth grade. Not in high school yet. That summer.

She heard that I was screwing a bunch of guys over on the point, across the bay.

Screwing a bunch of guys.

She had a boyfriend. He had an older brother. It was his older brother that told him. I don't know how much older, but I think around my older sister's age? Maybe older even? I don't know, but something I just remembered was that his family lived across the street from my grandmother. My grandmother's house was also my uncle's house.

I told my friend that he was lying. That he was telling a lie about me. That that, did not happen. I didn't do that.

She confronted him, in front of me, and that was when he said that his brother had heard that and told him that.

I said it was not true.

She broke up with him that night.

She remained my friend.

Years later, when I was thirty and had traveled back to that town with Chris to see the places that I was remembering, I called her. She still lives there and works in that town.

I told her I was remembering stuff. She told me that another friend of ours from high school had told her something similar.

It was about some younger guys and some sort of sick group/cult they were a part of. I don't remember all the details, but I do remember thinking that this means there was another generation of this. That it was still going on at this point, thirty years later.

I am so, so frightened of this memory, if indeed this is a memory.

The abortion means I was involved and raped up to my thirteenth/fourteenth birthday. I have no visual memory of this.

Only the story from my friend.

And my memory of the abortion.

Why am I so afraid? I've seen so many
awful things already. So many. Really awful
things. Horrific. Beyond comprehension.

How could it be that I came through this
whole and caring and capable of
compassion? Of love?

What else happened?

What did my uncle do to me, and why? It
looks as if he was involved at every age.
Every age I was. From two to fourteen.

Every age.

He was at the rituals. He took me in his car
to other men. He took me and my baby
sister to a ritual. He raped me in the liquor
store. My uncle. My uncle. My godfather.

These memories encompass my entire
childhood.

My conscious mind has no image or recall
of him in my childhood.

Yet now, as I remember these things, he was
a huge part. He played a huge part of every
aspect of this story. My sister saw him do
these things. In my home.

What am I not remembering?

I keep thinking of my uncle.

I keep thinking of the beach. The stories of what went on across the bay. Stories of me. Me screwing a bunch of guys. That's how my friend heard it. Clearly drugs were involved if this story has any merit, because I have no conscious memory of it. Yet it keeps creeping in now.

That, and my uncle.

I see him strutting with an erection in my house, in my hallway outside of my bedroom when I was two years old. Strutting with black pants on. He would have been sixteen then. Sixteen. I was two. My older sister was there.

Strutting.

When I first had the memory, I did not identify him as my uncle. I was confused. I knew it wasn't my father but didn't know who it was. Only that he was young, handsome, and looked familiar. He looked like family. But the block of my uncle was so strong that I didn't see him clearly, didn't even recognize him.

Now he's everywhere.

My father's youngest brother.

What am I afraid to see?

What am I afraid to see?

What am I afraid of?

What happened across the bay? At the point?

Was I taken on a boat? What? How come I have no memory of this? No recall?

How come it was a total shock when she told me the story?

An abortion???

Did I have an abortion?

What don't I want to see?

My head hurts now. The left side of my head hurts. Above my left eye. It hurts.

I woke up covered in sweat because of something. Something is there. Is here. It wants to be seen. Recalled. Recorded.

It's a missing piece of this puzzle that is my childhood. My family. My godfather.

My head hurts.

It throbs.

Later that same morning, I've begun to see some things.

At first, I saw my hands tied together. I was in a boat. In the bow (I think) of a boat.

I see light glinting off of dark water.

My hands tied together. I'm lying in a boat. My head is leaning on something. Something white.

I'm curled up. My legs are not tied together.

Then I start to remember scenes, pictures, images. They begin to form a story. I did this without writing it, by allowing the images to come.

Here are the things I saw, the things I recall.

I see me walking on a road. I see the gravel. I have sandals on. Dark leather sandals. Blue jeans. A reddish sleeveless shirt.

I see my father's jeep pull up. There is an older man in the front of it with him. There are two or three younger men in the back.

I'm told to get in, so I do. It's my father. I'm terrified of my father.

I have sort of a sense of where this was but not exactly. Not too far from the house.

I am told to drink something. It is a lot. It is in a white cup. It is yellow.

My hands are tied together. As I am remembering this, my heart is beating faster and faster and faster. I become increasingly afraid.

Something is tied around my mouth so I can't scream. I am terrified. I do not know these men. They are younger.

When we stop, it is at the dock. The dock of the Lodge which is right around the corner from my home. It is a fancier dock and has a light and benches. It is more expensive to dock there.

The biggest guy picks me up and carries me. He is young, stocky, square; like a linebacker. He carries me to the dock and into the boat. He steps in the boat carrying me.

My father stands by the jeep and watches. And the other, older man.

I am laid down in the boat. This is where the image was from. The lights from this dock shining on the dark water. The river was always sort of murky.

I don't' know how late it was. By the time the boat reaches the point it was pretty dark.

I can hear the water lapping against the metal boat. It is a familiar sound and it lulls me. My heartbeat slows down as this memory proceeds. Things get fuzzier.

It is a small boat.

The fire looks large. The point where we shore up is a rocky one. Isolated in a way. You wouldn't go there normally because of the rocks. It's not real comfortable. It looks dark.

I am picked up and sort of handed out of the boat. I don't' know if I can't walk because of the drugs or because my ankles are now also tied together.

In total there are five, maybe seven men. Young men. I am lying down now, but I see them across the fire. There is a dark haired one who seems to be running things.

They are young, in their twenties.

They pass a bottle of some sort of liquor from left to right and they all drink from it. It is dark, the liquid is dark or the bottle.

It is some sort of ritual.

Some sort of ritual with these men.

This is all I remember now.

This is enough for now.

I have to stop.

It's 2:26 in the morning. This is the second, or maybe the third time I've woken up tonight. Something is still eating at me, keeping me awake. I believe it's a memory. Maybe more of that most recent recall on the beach.

I'm going to quiet my mind and see what shows up. I'd really like to get some sleep. I'm exhausted.

What I see now is this: (There is an image here, I've sketched it with stick figures.)

I seem to fade in and out as I lay there. Some sort of colored powder is thrown into the fire and it changes color. These guys are not in robes. Regular clothes.

I am laying on my side.

They say things together. It's not chanting, but repetitive and building in intensity. Building in volume.

These guys are fucking sick. It's going to be some sort of gang rape. I don't know what they are saying, but they are getting each other very excited; shaking their heads and yelling.

This is a True Story

The dark-haired guy says/yells "Bring me the virgin!" It is very loud and this gets my attention. (I had been drowsy, staring at the fire.)

The big guy, the one who carried me into the boat, now picks me up. I am then carried around to the other side of the fire and laid on my back, directly behind the dark-haired guy.

The big guy then takes my sandals and jeans off. I have no will or ability to fight this. I am sort of like a rag doll. My hands are untied and lay at my side.

A blindfold is tied now around my eyes, so that I don't see any faces.

As this is being done, they are yelling and there is movement, like they are standing up or something. Now is where I just don't know by seeing what is happening. I feel pushed around and entered over and over. Rolled over at one point.

I do not see anything but feel pushed down into sand and rocks.

Just a piece of meat.

The next part I remember is being lifted up and the big guy is stepping into the boat. Somehow, my clothes are on, I can see, I am still gagged with the cloth and that is so uncomfortable. I see the fire in the distance and the men there. They are still excited somehow, but not as loud. Patting each other on the back. I see them pass a bottle or something to each other.

I am now laying in the back of the boat and I cannot see anything. It is colder, darker. The ride is bumpy and I feel the bumps. I also feel a bit sore and disheveled. My hands are bound.

I am becoming alert. I see lights now. The boat is back at the dock. The big guy has been sitting near to where I was laying down (in the bottom of the boat). He leans over and takes the rope away from my wrists. It was a white rope.

I look at him then. He has lighter hair. A big square head. Light eyes, not unkind but sort of vacant. I don't know how to describe it.

This is a small boat. Not a cabin cruiser, a small ski boat.

He reaches under me and says "It's time to go. Do you think you can walk?"

I nod.

He carries me up and onto the dock and sets me down feet first.

We begin to walk towards the land. I see the Jeep then, towards the right. I see my father, and as we step off the dock, he turns and walks to the car and gets in and starts it.

The square guy stays with me and opens the passenger door for me.

I step up into the Jeep and it hurts a bit. It stings between my legs.

I have sandals on. I notice this when we were walking off the dock.

I don't hear my father say anything. But I hear the square guy say, "Here you go Mr. X, back in one piece."

My father says nothing.

The square guy shuts the passenger door.

My father backs the car up a bit and then drives away.

Home is around the corner.

I decided to see if I could put a more
precise time frame on that most recent
memory, at the point across the bay.

I got centered and told myself to see the
closest birthday to that event. My birthday
is a summer birthday, so it seems that it
would point me to a more specific year.

It took a while. At first, I saw nothing at all.
I have no conscious memories of birthdays
as a child. Only from pictures. My mother's
pictures.

The first thing I saw was the floor. It was
blue-green and dark. Large tiles. Square. Not
ceramic tiles, but institutional-like floor.
Not new.

I thought of my home, but I had no memory
of a floor like that.

Then I saw a table and chair legs. They were
metal (the legs). The seats themselves
looked tan.

It was daytime. Sun was streaming in
through the windows.

I thought of the fire house. I knew that this was on the second floor.

When I looked out from the end of the table, it was one of those long rectangle tables. Like cafeteria tables.

There were men there. One woman. I noticed later that it was Rachel.

There were probably 15 people there, give or take.

My mother was there, bustling about.

My father was there.

My little sister too, but she was not at the table. She was in the corner to my right, and sort of behind me.

She would have been ten.

It was my 13th birthday.

I see a cake, not candles, but with writing.

"Happy Birthday (and my name here)"

There are no flowers on the cake. There is a picture, small, in the left-hand corner of the cake. I can't make it out. The writing is in cursive.

This is a True Story

The cake is sort of in the middle of these people, these men. In order to read it I have to move my perspective away from where I am actually standing/sitting and walk behind the men.

This is some sort of rite of passage. It is more for them, for this organization, than for my birthday.

It is something, I suspect, that was done to "normalize" my childhood. To mark the fact that I now approached womanhood and this particular role in the cult had completed itself.

There was to be no more use of me, at least officially in the cult, in that way.

I notice a few things.

One guy stands out because he is smiling at me. Big smile.

It's the middle of the day.

My mother had to do this, to set this up, to organize this. I feel this.

It seems like more of a meeting than a birthday celebration.

These people are not familiar.

They are not wearing robes, but street clothes, all different, a few suits.

They don't care about me and even less about my parents.

This puts that gang rape on the point, in my 13th year. I turned 13 that summer.

I drew a picture here, with stick figures, of what it is I remember.

Below the picture I wrote:

"I don't know how to comfort that little girl. What does she want/need? How can I help her?"

"I'm crying, it's all I want to do. Gang raped at 13. Offered up by my father. WTF."

I had another memory. It began with a pressure on the left side of my head. Sort of like a veil or something was pressing down there, making things fuzzy, making it hard to concentrate.

So, I decided to see what it was.

When I looked at the floor, I saw a white tile floor. The tiles were large, rectangular, sort of shiny.

The walls were light golden-brown paneling.

They were glistening.

There were no windows.

My perspective was such that to my left and behind me there was a door. To my left and in front of me was a woman; brown, dark hair, round chubby sort of face, dark eyes. I can only see the eyes and a bit of hair. She is not tall, seems cheerful. I see blue - scrubs. She is wearing scrubs and a mask so I only see her eyes. Her hands are wearing gloves, rubber gloves.

I see a shiny metal table. It is rectangular. It is what I am sitting on.

I see the shiny table, the glistening wall in front of me, the blue of the scrubs.

Someone else walks in and it is a man. He is to my left now. I barely see him. He has glasses, gold rimmed and square/rectangular. He has sandy hair. He is somber. I don't hear him say anything.

I see the woman, the cheery woman. I have my legs spread and strapped with some sort of leather strap to the end of the metal table. The metal table I am sitting on.

I see a sort of instrument. It resembles this: (Here I have drawn what looks sort of like a long handled skinny butter knife that is not round, but rectangular and curved at the end.)

It is long and slightly curvy. Metal and shiny with a long handle.

Somehow, I know that there is going to be a scraping. A scraping of the inside of me.

This is to be done by the man with the glasses who I assume is a doctor.

While it happens, the round-faced woman stays up by my face and torso. She is holding me down with her arms.

I do not perceive this as harmful or harsh even. I am feeling like I was drugged. There is no pain.

I see blood now. A large splat of blood. It is on a blue cloth that was placed on the table between my legs.

I don't remember getting cleaned up. I don't remember how I got there or how I left there.

I do have a sense it was happening in that house. In Rachel's house. The basement was to the right as you looked at the house from the front door. This room was in the basement.

I figure now that this was an abortion. The only word that came to me when I recalled it was "scraping". I don't know what I was told or that I knew I was pregnant. I do not believe so.

I know that I was thirteen when I got my "first" period, and in the eighth grade. This was before my fourteenth birthday and before high school began.

What I put together now is that I was still being used in the pedophile ring until I came up pregnant, before my first menses. This would place the abortion in the year 1972.

Once it was performed, I was no longer useful in the pedophile ring, because I was not supposed to be a "breeder".

That was not the deal.

The memory of the cult ritual where I was about fourteen and had the green robe involved, probably happened after this abortion.

I suspect that it was then that I was to be put to use for something else inside the cult.

I suspect that I would have had to participate or "help" at this point.

I suspect that I never did.

For an abortion to take place in a sanitary and successful and secretive fashion in 1972 must have cost a fortune.

I have not fully processed this emotionally.

Although I've been with women when they made the decision about whether or not to have an abortion, I've always felt that it was something I could never do myself. This was not an opinion I ever shared with anyone.

I did not consciously make a decision to have an abortion at the age of thirteen, and knowing now that it has happened to me, to this body and to this fetus, is tough to make any logical sense of.

I'm not sure where to put it.

What I did do is love, bless and release her (the fetus) and tell her that she is free of any negative emotion or guilt or harm that was stuck to that event. She can move on to other lifetimes and better circumstances.

The only other thing I have to say about this is that when I first saw a gynecologist for my cycle, and was examined, he told me that I had a "tilted uterus". I never knew what that meant.

He never told me that he saw evidence of an earlier pregnancy or abortion.

This is a True Story

Some new things.

I put these pieces into a pile and see what fits, what fits together.

I try to make sense of these pieces. These things that don't make sense. Not to me.

Yesterday I felt as if I was choking. I couldn't get any air.

Then I began to see, and here is what I saw:

My legs are skinny. I am not little. I have bare legs. Keds. White, but dirty and I don't see any laces. Bare legs under a robe.

My robe is purple.

We are outside. Remote. Quiet. Big area. Field. Earthy smell. Dirt, hay/grass smell.

I walk on ground, not floor. Buildings are far away.

My godfather is to my left. A woman, older than me but not too much older than me, is standing on my right. Her robe is deep purplish red. My godfather's robe is green.

My mother and my father are behind me, a way back. Their robes are purple for her and green for him.

Directly in front of me is the scary man in the black robe.

Note – I did a bit of research into the colors of robes. This is what I found online, under   Satanic Ritual and Anton LaVey:

Black/white/red are the primary colors of Satanic Ritual

Red is fire, anger, blood, sexual desire, aggression, Mars

Green is Venus, Earth, Wealth, Monetary Benefit

Indigo/Violet is Neptune, Vision, Unconscious, Sacrifice, Psychic

Black is Saturn, Death, Curse, Destruction, Most Powerful, Hides & creates confusion

So, we all walk and follow the black robed man, like in formation. We walk to these points and stop at each one. Is there five? I am not sure the number.

I see people trussed up, tied, knees up, hands around legs. Are they dead? How old are they? Not babies, older. I don't see them clearly.

I have to go to each one.

It's a progression. Go to one, do something, go to another, do something. It's not clear in my mind what I do, but it involves chopping.

The name of the ceremony begins with a "T" or has a "T" in it. "Transference"? "Transformation"? "Transcendence"? (These are just guesses)

I feel robotic in this memory. I feel no emotion. But I have a sense of a rite of passage. From childhood to adulthood maybe. Adulthood in the cult. Adulthood in the cult.

Things are chopped off. Toes?

I don't know.

Then, after going to all the points, the points where the bodies are trussed up, I take the things, or some of the things (because there are too many for me to carry), I take them and walk.

The circle of red robes opens up. It is beyond the black robed man. In another section. Closer to the buildings maybe?

After we walk the Pentagram, we go to the red robes.

Only I walk in. It opens up. I go in the middle.

Things are put around me. Maybe ingested.

I lay down. I also see myself on my knees.

I don't see any more now.

I have drawn a picture of this, but the placement is not exact.

I feel nothing really.

Just seeing things.

Putting pieces together.

This is a True Story

I mentioned my sister. Was she there? My older sister?

I don't think so.

It was a rite of passage. A rite of passage.

There was a cult. My father was their butcher.

His mother sold herself for sex/money. (This was due to poverty, not the cult.)

Very poor. Dirt poor.

My mother gave me to anyone and everyone for sex.

I remember:

Rape in a liquor store at 8 years old. Several men. Rode my bike to get there.

A blue gown - for a princess who was given to a prince.

Little red riding hood and a wolf.

Child trafficking + Satanic Cult + Uncle + Father

Everyone in that town

Never go back.

I cannot go back.

I have to remember. Such a word, an impossible word. It cannot be done physically. You cannot RE-MEMBER someone.

Remembering happens in the mind, in the brain only. Once dismembered you can only be sewn back together, or something.

The Funeral Home. I wonder about that. Did the bodies come from there, or from him (the owner) because he had access to bodies?

His father was in it. Ran the funeral home. Then, the son. He got Alzheimer's very young. He's dead now.

Dead.

I wonder if the trussed-up bodies in my latest recall were dead?

This was not a place I was familiar with. It was further away. It was desolate though.

The land was far away from the barn, the barns, the buildings. Two or three of them, gray or blue, light. Maybe dingy white?

I see my feet. I see my feet. I see my feet.

They are young woman's feet. Young. Woman.

Teenager? How old was I?

I see my feet and I see the robe swirling around my feet. They are on dirt; it is matted with hay? Hay or grass. It smells earthy, but it is windy. The robes swirl.

Here I have drawn another depiction of what I remember.

Red robes open up the circle, and I go in the middle. It feels like only two go with me. My uncle and the dark red robed younger woman.

But I can't really see them once I'm in there. I only see me.

I'm becoming very confused about the robe color. When I look down into the center of the circle at me, it is GREEN. The robe has changed color and it is green now. The things on my body as I lie there are on a green robe.

A green robe.

The kneeling me is in a green robe. Dark green.

I'm very confused.

I don't remember changing robes.

This feels like a larger coven, many people, further away from my town.

It's a large piece of land. Remote. I wonder if I smell the sea. I'm not sure.

I don't know precisely the place where the scary black robed dude goes or where my parents end up.

But I think it looked like this (here I've drawn another depiction).

I wrote "I think at some point I am alone in the circle of robes." Also, an arrow pointing between my parents with this, "I almost want to put white between them, here, but that happens after."

Who is the dark red robed woman? Who is she?

I feel a sense of her more than I see her. I said my sister, but no, she has dark hair and is, I think, younger than my sister. But at this point, my sister would be in her early twenties and off to college.

This woman. I only see dark hair and a dark red robe.

Is she, my handler? I don't know what a handler is, but there is a sense of ownership from her, as if I am her charge.

I am what she takes care of and guides. Like, she shows me things. Shows me what to do.

The female version of ownership.

My godfather, the male version. Maybe.

He raped me from the time I was an infant, a baby.

He's older than my sister.

Was he more things than I realize now?

The prince?

The Wolf?

There were costumes.

This is a True Story

Sick. Sick. Sick. Sick. Sick.

Early this morning I recalled something.

It is further detail about something I'd remembered earlier.

It was so very vivid. Right now, as I write this, my heart beats so very fast. My left hand is scrunched into a fist and I'm covering my mouth. I am clammy.

This is absolutely terrifying.

I feel ill.

I feel as if I have to tell this part here. To document my remembering it. You see, I'm really, really good at blocking things; hiding them away so that I can function.

If I write this down, it will be real again, despite how many places I try to hide it.

My left hand is still scrunched into a fist.

It is as if I am afraid that I'll scream.

Here goes...

This makes clearer a memory of what I imagine was my last cult ritual.

I was older.

I've spoken of this before; the ritual was huge. My uncle was there. My parents. My handler. The scary man in the black robe.

Part of the detail, you'll see, is the programming. It includes what I was told. It includes intuitive detail of what they wanted me to believe.

It was outside.

A huge field.

In front of me is a pentagram. It is not contiguous, but five separate points, the points on the star. These points are made of wood. They look like this:

(There is an image I have drawn in a notebook.)

Each point is made of two large planks of wood. They are joined together. They are placed in the shape of the pentagram in the field, outside.

I didn't "see" them the first time I recalled the ritual.

I only saw people. I only saw people trussed up and placed in a shape, in the shape of the pentagram.

I saw that today as well.

Yet today, I also saw what happened first.

I need to say here that when I recalled this today, I nearly lost it. I was crying and curling up and my body hurt. My head hurt, above my left eye for some reason, and I felt sick; so, so sick.

It was outside.

I was standing in the midst of that pentagram. At first, I was in front of it, next to it - but I saw it.

I saw the pentagram. I saw the people. The people were making the pentagram.

They were lying with their heads faced towards the middle, tilted up. They were seeing each other and their heads were lying between the point, the inside of the point of the pentagram. Their heads were held up because their arms were pulled up and back so that they made a V, and they were attached to the wood of the pentagram.

They were naked.

Their legs were also shackled to the earth. Their legs were spread. This is what it looked like:

(Another drawing)

Only their neck is angled so that the head tilts forward.

Their mouths were covered. I think some sort of cloth was tied around their mouth, tied in the back of their head.

It was so they couldn't scream.

I think now this was for security reasons. I do not know if I was told that.

I only see clearly one man. He is to my right and a bit forward. He is young. Dark hair.

I sense it is not symmetrical. They are not all the same size and not all men and not all young.

I recall then, the story.

It is the programming. The story I was told.

Each of the five represented a member of my family or a friend – someone I cared about.

I recalled someone represented my grandmother, my brother. Those are the definite ones in my memory of this.

Yet some of the pentagram is still foggy – blurry – I don't see any other faces. But I know that they represent people specific to ME, people I cared about.

I was told I was BAD, BAD, BAD. I was evil and so evil that I would kill even the people I loved to save myself or help myself. I was told over and over how evil I was.

Some of this gets blurry. This could be due to the drugs, yet truly, at this point, it is not a precise visual.

I suspect the people staked to the ground were drugged as they were too docile. I see fear in that one man's dark eyes.

The people all have white skin.

I see white hair on an older woman.

I believe I see a child.

I have to kill them. I recall killing the man.
At some points, I leave my body.

My viewpoint is from above the field.

There is someone standing on the opposite
side of the man. Opposite from me.

He holds a stick.

The killing weapon is a long stick and at its
end is a point. The point is made of metal
and has like razor edges all around and
they are serrated.

It is made that way to kill with pain.

This is sort of the idea, only sharper.
(Another picture)

It is supposed to be twisted.

Twisted for tortuous pain.

The other thing I recall is that it was not an
orderly process. I don't recall if I held the
stick for every killing or just that man.

I do recall that part of the terror game was
that the people in the pentagram didn't
know who would be killed next. That is why

their heads were tilted up in the points of the star. They watched me. They watched each other get killed.

I felt frenzied. I'd say I was drugged. It was so surreal. I was in and out of body as this went on.

At the end, they are all dead.

I see myself holding the stick and there is blood on my hands and arms and on the stick.

I don't know who did all of the killings.

The next part is what I had already recalled.

Somehow, I'm in a green robe now.

The people are trussed up. Sitting with their backs in the angle/point of the pentagram, facing the middle.

Now I am holding a long, big knife sort of thing. It is huge.

(Another picture)

I have to cut off their toes, or a toe.

It is an offering. Proof of my evil. A trophy of my killing.

It is once they are collected that I go to the center of the larger circle. I take the trophy toes to the black robed scary dude.

I think the larger circle of people were there the whole time, surrounding the pentagram.

My uncle is to my left. That woman (the handler) is to my right. My parents are behind me.

That's what I recalled today.

I woke up.

There are things to remember.

The cup I am holding is huge. It warms my hand and reminds me of comfort, of my children and grandchildren. It reminds me how much I love them.

What is weird is that I don't really know love -

Love is not a commodity.

Love is an intrinsic response to something of value - to truth - to essence.

I have value.

I didn't learn this. It is something I am only now realizing, feeling.

I feel, right now, a sort of truth in my body.

I used to feel just big and square and ugly and reliable. It was my fallback gesture.

To do what was asked of me.

Every time. Every time. Every time.

Never refuse.

If you refuse, bad things happen. If you don't do what you are told, bad things happen.

What bad things?

They will kill you.

They will hurt you.

They will rip off your arms and your legs, cut them off or rip them off while you have to watch.

You have to watch so you'll know what it feels like. So, you'll know how to do it when it is your turn. Your turn to do it.

What?

What?

What?

Your turn to do it.

You have to do it. You have to follow orders. The ones who scream the loudest are the ones who didn't follow the rules. You have to do it the right way, or they will kill you.

They will kill you.

They will kill you.

They always kill.

It is part of what they promise.

First, they hurt.

They hurt so you know what it is like to be killed, so you know you did the wrong thing.

The wrong thing.

(This next part is printed and much smaller…)

You cannot yell.

You cannot talk.

You cannot look away.

Don't move. Don't move. Don't shut your eyes or they will see. They will force them open or take them out.

You have to watch.

You have to watch the killing. You have to hear.

This is a True Story

You have to hear the screaming. It is the loudest when you don't comply. They take longer then, so it hurts more.

So, you get the message.

The message of obey. Obey. Obey.

Do what you are told to do.

Don't cry or they will notice you.

If they notice you, it is bad.

(Now here, again, it is in longhand.)

It is time to remember. It is time to remember the bad thing.

Who did the bad thing?

It was him. It was my father.

He did the butchering. He knew how.

He always did it the best. He was a hunter. He knew how to clean his kill.

All of these thoughts are coming now...coming so fast.

So fast.

Sick. Sick. Sick. Sick. Sick.

He was part of it.

It was his job to clean the kill.

It was his job. He knew how to do it with pain, or quickly. He hated it but he did it.

He did it because he had to. It was his job.

His job.

He was my father.

The Butcher.

If I was quiet and complied, he wouldn't have to kill me.

But he had to kill and only if I was quiet would he not kill me.

I was only an asset if I was quiet, if I did what they wanted.

What did they want?

They wanted always quiet. They wanted always access.

This is a True Story

Always about the business. The business down there. That was the big deal.

They liked to put things in.

In me.

In my openings. My holes.

I had holes that they put things in; things of theirs.

My father liked this too.

My father liked the business down there.

My business.

My father was there because of what he liked. My father was there because of what he could do. He could do a clean kill.

He liked it. He liked children.

I don't know what any of this means. I am not remembering anything specific. It is all jumbled.

It is all jumbled now.

Dark. People. Screaming. My father.

Somehow there is a feeling that he is victimized by it too. It makes no sense. He doesn't have to kill me because of what I can do; what I do.

What is it that I do?

It is about the business. The business down there.

The private business that is not private at all.

I feel little now. Not big and square but little. Little and pretty and scared.

I am confused. My parts hurt. My private parts, they just hurt all the time.

It is their fault.

It is his fault.

It is his fault.

It is his fault.

He was the grown-up.

He was my father. He was supposed to care. He was supposed to protect me; to keep me from harm.

He did no such thing.

What he did instead is put me in harm's way and use me. I was a piece of garbage. Property...useful only for the business.

Useful so that he wouldn't have to kill me.

If I did as I was told, I didn't have to be killed.

I had to watch. I had to let them do their weird things down there.

It hurt sometimes. It hurt a lot.

I could not move, but sometimes I was hurt. Moved around. It was like I wasn't there. Like I was necessary but irrelevant. Those words make no sense in a single sentence.

What I want to do is remember. Remember being me. How did I feel?

Shamed. Scared. Terrified. Irrelevant, but necessary. Confused. Always a victim, never in charge.

There was no love. I was always afraid. Always afraid.

It could happen at any time. I could be taken somewhere.

I could be told to do something.

I could be raped.

That's what it was. It was rape. I may not have fought, but it was rape.

I was trained to not fight or they would kill me.

My father would kill me.

I ran away once. And they called him to come and get me. He never said a word.

I don't know what I told them but he never said a word, all the way home. Off of a fucking island. On a ferry. Not a word. I was terrified.

I was sixteen then.

Even then, not remembering, I knew. Knew enough to be terrified.

I don't know if I ever told anyone. I don't know if I actually told that nun in first grade. I'd like to think that I did, but a big part of me says "no - you didn't". You know what happens if you fight back. It only hurts more and they kill you anyway.

It is like I had two choices: comply or die.

The other stuff, the business end of things, that was awful and hurt and annoying and weird.

The killing was something else again.

They will kill you.

You have to know this.

They are not averse to killing. People. Old men. Ladies. Children. Mostly children.

They had to chase them first. They were non-compliant and had to run and be chased before being eaten. It was a game.

I was not eaten. I was not chased. I did not run. I was quiet. I was not killed.

I stayed alive.

The business was the price I paid for life.

How do I feel now?

I don't know. I was a child.

<u>NO MORE.</u>

I have seen love.

I do not have to say yes.

I choose only love, demonstrable love. This is not (*found in*) my family. My family of origin.

This is a True Story

Adult Reflections

This is a True Story

I keep hearing about asking that part of me that is coming forward to step aside, so that I can see who is hiding. There are a few.

One hates everything about her life. She does not feel love or loved. She feels replaceable – by anyone or anything that offers something better. She is, she feels, irrelevant. She doesn't matter.

The other is in shock. Terrified. She cannot pretend or move. She just wants to sit very still and have nothing asked of her. She can't feel.

What do I do?

If I ask the first one to step aside, what will happen?

She feels cold, hateful. She could care less, really. She is exhausted.

If she steps aside, what is left?

If she lets go of her anger, if she steps aside...who comes out?

(Here there is a drawing of a long-haired girl with the word "angry" below her. Next to that is a drawing of a large face with tears

streaming down it, and the word "sad"
below it.)

This next part was printed very large:

CAN SHE STEP ASIDE?

NO. THERE IS NO ONE BENEATH HER.

BUT THERE IS.

**NO. SHE HATES, DESPISES HER LIFE.
THERE IS <u>NO</u> LOVE IN IT. THERE IS ONLY
REQUIREMENT.**

**SHE MUST OBEY, IN ORDER TO KEEP HER
HOME, HER SOURCE OF INCOME, HER
WAY OF LIVING.**

SHE MUST OBEY.

**THERE IS NO REAL FEELING BENEATH
THE HATRED.**

IT IS SO <u>COLD</u>.

**YOU DON'T CARE ABOUT ME. IT'S ALL
SELFISHLY MOTIVATED. I AM ONLY AS
GOOD AS WHAT I CAN PROVIDE.**

CAN YOU STEP ASIDE FOR A MOMENT?

(There was no answer, only the following written on the next page.)

WHEN THE COLD COMES

IT IS AN ICE SHIELD

WITHOUT IT, I AM VULNERABLE

WITHOUT IT, I AM EXPOSED

WITHOUT IT, I AM HURT

I DON'T WANT THE HURT

I DON'T WANT TO FEEL

THERE IS ONLY PAIN

IT IS ALL EXPOSED WITHOUT THE SHIELD

I CAN'T.

SHE TRUSTS ME

SHE DOESN'T WANT THE PAIN

WHAT CAN SHE DO WITHOUT HER
SHIELD?

Physical withdrawal came as a shock on May 28th. It hit hard, with violent shaking and profuse sweating. There were continual fevers, headaches and sleepless nights, 24/7. Eventually I took a constant stream of Acetaminophen and Ibuprofen to fend off the shakes long enough so that I could get a few hours' sleep at a time. This first acute phase lasted until June the 8th, a full 12 days.

On the 13th day I woke after a full night's sleep in sort of shock. It was the first time I'd felt any benefit from this physical withdrawal process. I felt new. I felt a bit empty. I felt whole in a way I had never felt. I got in the car for the first time that morning, and cried as I drove. I felt free. I couldn't wait to start my new life in this chain-free body.

The sleeping through the night lasted for just two nights. I suspected, at first, that I had over-done it physically. I was so, so happy to feel human again that I did a whole bunch of things that were physical. I was elated.

The third night I again awoke drenched with sweat and violently shivering. There were another two days of intense withdrawal symptoms. I took it easy this time. Sleeping as much as I am able to during the day and not pushing it with work.

The "over-did" it was a fallacy. On day # 16 I realized that I did, in fact, relapse.

Emotional addiction in our body turns into powerful physical addiction, similar to Heroin. What happened was in the 3 days before the sweats and convulsions began again, I had received, and read, a hand written note, an email and a text from my siblings. I did not respond to them. I deleted them from my phone and laptop. I thought that was enough to prevent any toxic effect of contact with the family.

After 2 days of intense fevers and shaking, I began to understand what was happening. I could not have *any* connection with the family. None. Anything received from them, and read by me, only sets up the chemical cocktail in my brain again, the one I am addicted to. It is the chemical of fear and adrenaline. It is well concealed beneath the desire to belong, to be loved, to be part of people who share my name and who look like me; to be part of a family. I thought that by NOT responding, and just observing, I would be removed enough to continue to heal. I was wrong.

Once I realized what was happening, I blocked everyone in my family of origin from my phone and email accounts. There will be no more unexpected texts or electronic mail or phone calls. It was late last night when I did this, and when I went to bed, I was still running a fever. I woke up after about 5 to 6 hours sleep, an enormous length of time! I was not running a fever and it was hours past the time that I would have been due to take some Acetaminophen.

That is validation enough for me. Emotional addiction is insidious and persistent and hides beneath sentiments like "doing the right thing" and "being nice" and "staying in touch". In order for me to heal, and rid myself of this addiction, I have to go cold turkey for now. This means no contact at all. No *hint* of contact. It is the only way. Like an alcoholic, I will have to avoid being around those people who inspire the desire for the chemical/drug. That would be my family of origin.

I was unprepared for the strength of this chemical addiction. Clearly it controlled me for sixty years. It is the only thing I knew, what I considered "normal". It is everything but.

I have done some research and spoken to my counselor about what is going on for me. What this is, is a release of toxic emotions that have held my brain hostage and in fear for my entire life. This abuse began before I could walk, which was at 15 months of age. It is a massive release of adrenaline and fear; the chemicals I produced for survival. They are what's kept me alive until now.

Like any addiction, the trick for me now is to NOT GO BACK to believing that I am in danger, that everyone is out to get me, and that I must do what anyone/everyone asks of me. I also must NOT EVER GO BACK to the source of this addiction, i.e., my family of origin.

I learned to live like that, in a state of fear, before I could talk. I was in constant terror. The reality of this physical reaction to my process of remembering and healing from my childhood of horrors, only serves to validate it all for me. Emotions turn into chemicals in our brain. As I release the chemicals, the emotions go as well.

It was not a surprise to my counselor that this physical withdrawal began, but it was to me.

Everything I read about going through withdrawal from an addiction tells me that how long it takes depends on the length of time on the addictive substance. It also depends on whether or not there are setbacks, i.e., relapses. Estimates begin at two weeks. So far, it's been about 3 weeks. I don't know how long it takes to get rid of sixty years of fear and adrenalin, but I am determined that there will be no more reversions.

This is hard. I can barely walk at times. Everything hurts. I spend lots of time crying and moaning. Showers take place with me sitting on the bottom of the tub, too weak to stand. Yet above all of that I have one thought. It is "Move on out".

I've now cut off all contact with my family of origin. They are not asking why. I am not surprised.

Those 2 days of wholeness that I began to feel last weekend, were unlike anything I've ever experienced in this body during this lifetime. I actually recognized myself. When I look at the image of 3 or 5-year-old me, I no longer see a stranger, I can feel myself in her eyes.

When I began this process of remembering, I did so because I wanted to feel something. My deepest wish is that once I feel all of this pain, it will be time to feel the good stuff.

What occurs for me, after this recent relapse, is what this means for the recovery and rehabilitation of children who've been through something similar. I was pre-verbal when the abuse began, and the emotions that allowed me to survive an extremely toxic family situation turned into powerful addictions.

Are the children, once rescued from pedophile rings or satanic cults or child trafficking, being treated for their emotional dependence/compulsion? This withdrawal process is visceral and brutal and necessary *if I am to fully recover.* I would hope that the children's emotional situation is seen for what it is; a physical/chemical addiction.

I hear stories of both adult women and children returning again and again to severely abusive husbands, fathers and families. Talking therapy *will not* stop their actions. These are controlling chemicals that rule everything. My partner used to say that my impulse to visit my family of origin was sort of like "lemmings to the sea". Now I see what he means.

The story of lemmings, which is apparently not true, is that they cannot be stopped from jumping into the Arctic and drowning each year; a sort of mass suicide. This was a myth perpetuated by a Disney documentary, who actually threw them over the side a cliff to make the 1958 film.

As I proceed through this healing, I hope to offer insight into what is happening to me, both emotionally and physically. One of the reasons for this book is to raise awareness. The other is to assist in the recovery process of the many children and adults who've been through brutality and abuse, and lived to tell the tale.

It is 4:44 in the morning. I woke up an hour ago.

My mother. This is about my mother. The reality of all of this slowly, slowly, slowly settles. It settles very deep.

Then, I attempt to reconcile it with emotions, feelings, longings, pictures.

It does not fit together.

It's like someone took four 1,000-piece puzzles, threw them all in one box and said – this, right here, is your actual life. It is not just one picture with its many components. It is all four.

Puzzle number 1 is my mother's photo albums.

Puzzle number 2 is the satanic ritual abuse with my mother, my father, my uncle and others.

Puzzle number 3 is the pedophile ring with "Rachel" and my mother, father, uncle and others.

Puzzle number 4 is my older sister and my godfather and others.

If you notice, I have no puzzle. I have not had the ability to construct one of any coherence. It never, ever fit together as anything conclusive. If I had a box of pieces, they would be more nebulous. Made up of dreamy sorts of wishes and hazy sorts of memories. These would be interspersed with bits of terror, splashes of blood, and Sam.

It is the 17th day since physical withdrawal* began for me, and I am surrounded by thoughts of my mother. Things like, "How could anyone do that to another person?" quickly become "How could you, my own mother, do that to me, your daughter?"

The only answer that seems to be complete comes in the definition of sociopath.

My mother is a sociopath.

If you look up the definition of sociopath you'll see: "inability to put themselves in another person's shoes" and "almost no conscience, or not enough that it would change their behavior", and "looks to others only as a means to get what they want and "very charming" and "blames everyone else for their own behavior".

Let me tell you about my mother. Everyone, and I mean everyone, loves her. She is funny and charming and irreverent and very attentive. Any one of my friends who've met her, tell me "I love your mother". They all ask about her when we get together.

Her house is filled with pictures of family, friends and all of the trips that she went on with my father. Her closets are filled with well-made clothing. There are drawers and boxes of jewelry and cases of collectibles; plates and statues.

Then there are notebooks of unpaid debt and legal documents to handle these, just in case she dies before any of her children (me) or grandchildren (my sons and Sam's son) re-pay her in full. If that happens, these documents set legal payment up from my mother's estate to the rest of her children (anyone not me and who doesn't owe her any money).

In English, this means that if my mother was going to leave each of her children

$1,000.00 when she died, but I still owed her $500.00, that the $500.00 would be reduced from my inheritance and given to her other children. All nice and neat. Not weird at all.

That is my mother. She will be taking something from me, even after she's dead. What's ironic here is that, as you'll read, it is *in all probability* because of me and the services I supplied, that she has so many luxuries and so much money. I am sure money changed hands.

The other thing about my mother is that I've always considered her more of a friend than a mother. We could talk for hours. As I mentioned, she is very charming.

I felt connected to my mother.

It is surreal now to look at the actual relationship and put that connection piece in there. It is an actual component, along with everything else, yet it makes no sense.

It is only when you factor in how starving I was for anything that looked like love, that you can begin to see how it fits. As long as you agreed with my mother's narrative, she was delightful. It was especially wonderful if you were helping her with something. This was the role I chose most often.

You'd say that what I learned from my mother was that co-dependence meant love.

She has no backbone, and appears to be at the mercy of everyone and everything. It is never her fault.

I've never heard her say "no".

She complained to me about both of my sisters, seemingly at their mercy.

She consistently sends cards for every occasion, with a check enclosed if appropriate.

Somehow, I felt responsible for my mother - until now.

I wanted to alleviate all of her pain and make her happy. She once said to me, after I'd spent weeks with her helping her to heal from surgery, that "Now I know what it is to be loved."

So, how do any of those emotions fit with a mother who sold her daughter to a pedophile ring, and a Satanic Cult? All for what I've come to believe were "favors", lucrative "deals", and such?

It only fits if all of the pieces are thrown into one box – not fitting together, but resting nearby. All of them together were/are held in this brain of mine and always have been. It may not look cohesive or matched, yet they are only now coming together. All puzzle boxes combined into one image. Piecing them together is what this book is about.

* On 5.28 I began what can only be described as physical withdrawal symptoms. I was violently shaking, running fevers, couldn't walk or sleep or do much of anything. This is how withdrawal symptoms are defined by AmericanAddictionCenters.org:

The symptoms of drug withdrawal, and the length of that withdrawal, vary depending on the drug of abuse and the length of the addiction. These are a few withdrawal symptoms and timelines for major targets of abuse:

•Heroin and prescription painkillers: flu-like symptoms lasting an average of 5 days

•Benzodiazepines: anxiety and/or seizures lasting weeks or (in some cases) months

•Cocaine: depression and restlessness lasting 7-10 days

•Alcohol: tremors and/or seizures lasting three days to several weeks

These symptoms went on in an intense way for months, and are gradually tapering off as this book is being written.

What seems to have happened is that the need/drug of family dependence is so very strong, that my separating from it had an intense physical reaction, identical to a drug withdrawal. I took that drug *for sixty years.* It was a surprise to me when the symptoms showed up, yet not to my therapist. The only way to prevent a re-occurrence of severe shaking and other symptoms, is to maintain NO Contact.

This morning marks the first time that I've gone without Tylenol or Advil for a full 24 hours, in almost a month!!

No fever yesterday. June 20.

No sweats or shaking last night. June 20/21.

This is the first time since May 28th, which is a full 25 days of medicine, sweats, fevers, shaking, weakness, chills...

This is a milestone! Woo hoo!

I saw my therapist today.

He said he was struck by my clarity.

I feel as if something has been removed from my head. From the left side of my head, if that makes sense.

It's like waking up after sixty years of amnesia. There is room now. I can access what is going on around me without question. There is clarity. It is hard to describe.

I think that the car accident opened something up inside of me. It's been since then.

It's now been 48 hours without Advil or Tylenol.

Still waking up at night, twice. A little sweaty the first time, but no shakes or drenched clothes/pajamas/sheets and I went right back to sleep.

Today is Day # 26 since withdrawal began.

I've begun some physical exercise, yoga and weights, only about 15 minutes.

I am still very weak, out of breath quickly, taking the staircase one step at a time because of balance. So, I want to build up strength and muscle mass again.

I feel very clear, BUT there was a "CONTENT BLOCKED" message on my phone. I pressed it and then saw about a dozen from my sister, which has affected me.

From now on I am going to ask Chris to press it and delete them. I can't even see the names. It feels shitty.

My left foot is no longer black and blue.

All in all, I feel good today. I'm calling this improvement and healing and progress.

This is the third day in a row of no medicine – no Advil or Acetaminophen – and I slept through the night. This is a first.

I woke up only slightly sweaty/damp, but it was after 6+ hours of sleep. Close to 7 hours.

It felt great.

I did lots of chores and now I'm pretty much wiped out. I was hoping to plant some flowers today, but instead I'll be writing the book. I need to pace myself apparently.

So, I will do that.

Just plan one major thing each day for a while, and keep doing some exercises and stretches. Not every day, but every other day.

My feet, the bottoms of them, are achy. They hurt. I keep moving my toes back and forth to get the blood moving but I really don't know what is causing this. It's been going on for a while.

Last night I woke up time after time. It wasn't due to a fever.

I suppose it was just insomnia.

I think I'll stop being surprised by all of the different physical reactions and I'll take it one day at a time, one event at a time.

It will serve me better.

I exercised again today. #2

It felt good.

I showered too and I am thrilled to report that standing up while showering is now a regular thing, pretty much. It feels great. (I was unable to stand until now.)

I've re-structured some appointments so that there is no more than one thing each day. I am attempting to manage my life in a way that works. Works for me so I can function comfortably and feel success.

I am very fortunate to have Chris right now. He supports all of this. He supports me and is not hard to please.

There has been more detail added. I've put some pieces together.

This is a True Story

It is because of a dream. A dream where Chris and I were looking out a window in a door. I don't know the building but it wasn't this home, or any home I've lived in. Like an industrial building. We looked because of the commotion we heard. There was noise and, in the street and sidewalk through the glass door, there seemed to be babies everywhere.

Some of them dead or being killed or being pushed in strollers away from something or someone. Babies everywhere.

There were a few people hunched down on the curb, watching this and I suddenly throw my cell phone to them. It was that magical sort of dream-reality where the cell phone goes through the glass door, but the glass never breaks.

A man picks it up and walks away with it.

He had been one of the men crouched down on the curb, watching all of the babies and killing.

A thought goes through me that no one will be able to reach me now – how will family reach me? I need to get that phone.

Then, I am outside and asking where the man went, the man with my phone. They tell me he went that way, pointing to the right. I don't see him.

I wake up then and believe I've lost my phone. I start wondering how I'll get it back.

There is concern I feel, not panic. Eventually I remember it was a dream. I see my phone in the bedside table.

I believe the dream was about my brother and communication and blocking everyone and how that feels. I've been so conflicted.

(I decided that I had to block both phone numbers and email addresses from members of my family so that I don't ever see them and get triggered or set back or ill or experience extreme withdrawal symptoms. This is what I believe caused my recent set back, the seeing of all the text messages from my sister on my phone. It is now set up so that that won't happen.)

I've remembered a few more details and they tell me that the whole family/all of my siblings, to some degree had a part in this and have memories of this, even if they are not conscious memories.

This tells me to NOT make contact with any of them, once again, for safety reasons and also because I am in withdrawal.

I cannot take another sip of that family whiskey.

What I remembered today centers around my brother.

I've always remembered going to his room, as a two-year-old, after the men, after being with the men. The men in suits. Today there is more detail.

I was in a dress. It was tan. There was a design on it in red thread. It was a sundress. I had sandals on my feet.

I remember a man. He gave me an orange lollipop because I was a good girl. I was in his car. It was big. Not a station wagon.

I remember then some sort of parking lot or pull off, off to the side of the road. It is desolate, there are trees. Seeing it now, I'm reminded of the beach and the cliffs and all the places you can pull off, leave your car and head down to the water.

I feel as if I am picked up by my uncle here. Picked up and physically put in another vehicle, in the car that my uncle was driving.

Then the next memory is at my house. My brother comes out and helps me from my uncle's car/truck/van? Into the kitchen, through the side door.

My brother has his arm around me. He is skinny, but taller and sort of holding me up. He walks me to his room, his bed. I still have my lollipop. My orange lollipop. I fall asleep then.

This is a True Story

I remember there is noise/activity in my room. My room is right next to my brother and the one I share with Sam.

She would have been a baby.

My mother would have been taking care of her. She (my mother) did not work at the time.

I also recalled the time when my brother babysat me and Sam. He would have been about 12 years old. I would have been 6 then, and Sam 4.

He played a trick on us. He told us he heard a noise in the other room and that he'd go check. He told us not to follow. When he didn't come back, we went into the kitchen.

We found him on the floor. There was a big knife next to him and ketchup all over him and the floor.

Sam went nuts. Then he got up, and I think we were so happy he wasn't dead that we never got mad. It was weird though.

Now, I think that was his way of expressing some of what he'd been witness to. This is what my adult mine says about it, but I have not been told that by him or anyone else.

I believe all of my siblings saw something, participated in something. I don't know exactly what.

I will never mention this out loud. The last time I did, they killed my godmother to set an example, to send a message.

She was run over in broad daylight by a Mack truck.

My father drove to the place where it happened, right after it happened. They were sending him a message. That is now crystal clear.

I won't send cards or cash checks or open gifts or respond to any of them, in any fashion. Right now, this seems to be the safest and most successful way for me to get through this withdrawal and healing.

I will heal.

This is a True Story

I will heal.

The insomnia comes and goes. I am on the couch again, because most nights I can't sleep. There are some sweats still happening.

At some point I looked at my blocked calls again. I saw all the names, my brother, my sister. This is what set me back. It is like taking another drink; an addiction.

No more. I believe I've found a way in settings on my phone to prevent any notifications of blocked calls or blocked text messages. That should handle the temptation to look.

It is a strange thing to long, even now, for some sort of recognition from them.

Even now.

It's been referred to as "Stockholm Syndrome" and it's true. It is almost by impulse. I have to kick the habit and just *not go there.*

It's clear that now that I've remembered so much, *that everyone knew.* On some level, everyone in my family of origin knew.

I don't know what they remember now. But I CANNOT HAVE CONTACT WITH MY FAMILY. PERIOD. I AM ADDICTED. I CAN NEVER GO BACK. IT IS DEADLY FOR ME. DEADLY.

I MUST GET PAST THIS NOW. GET PAST THESE PHYSICAL SYMPTOMS OF FEVERS AND SWEATS AND GET ON WITH MY ACTUAL HEALING AND RECOVERY.

I'm still taking Ibuprofen occasionally or Acetaminophen occasionally or both, due to fevers and sweats. This will stop with no contact.

It's been about a week now since I saw the names (on my phone).

I will not go back there.

I have a plan for how to handle any USPS mail. Chris will read it and decide. I have a plan for how I will handle any emergency or death that I am made aware of through contacting Chris. I will stay off the radar by sending flowers. No contact.

I even have a plan for the inevitable circumstance of my mother's estate settling.

I will not physically engage with any of it. They can sell it at an auction. I don't care. I *cannot* go back there. I want nothing from her.

This is how I beat this addiction.

This is how I heal. No contact.

Do not worry about whatever stories they tell themselves about why. This must happen if I am to heal.

I will beat this addiction.

I want to record more of this withdrawal process that I am experiencing. Three days ago, I began to get the shakes. It was a complete surprise. It happened while I was out at Costco and I managed to get my groceries and even some gas before getting home.

I then began again to take the Ibuprofen and Acetaminophen regimen. I slept and shook for the rest of that day and the next.

Last night I again sweat through my pajamas, but the shakes didn't come, and today I've done a bit of gardening and shopping. There are no more withdrawal symptoms. I'm just tired.

I think what has triggered it, is my acceptance of my true history.

Several stand-out moments are when Chris told me what his parents did on two pivotal occasions during his upbringing. Both times they were compassionate with him, caring and protective. *I never knew what that looked like, or felt like.*

The other was this video I watched in which a newborn twin is failing until she's put in the incubator with her stronger twin sister, who immediately reaches out and puts her arm across her tiny shoulders.

That just cemented something in my brain that says... *You had a little sister who you tried to protect. You have a big sister who abused you and pimped you out to her friends.*

I've begun to accept the reality of my childhood. I don't know all of it, or remember all of it, but the fact that it happened is indisputable. I believe that these withdrawal symptoms are being triggered differently this time; by my own acceptance of the truth.

It seems that they are lasting shorter periods of time; if this is the third day and it is already subsiding.

It's hard because it's unexpected. When I stay on the regimen though (Acetaminophen and Ibuprofen) I can fend off any surprises.

I'm looking at this as progress.

One of the things I keep re-playing in my mind is that I really do know my family. I know each of them really intimately and when I think about that – my mother disgusts me, I've never liked my older sister and I was always afraid of my father. My brother I've always felt couldn't protect me and although he was kind to me at most times, he also knew on some level what was happening. I haven't reconciled that yet. Maybe there is more to remember.

In the ten years I was absent from the family he didn't reach out once, except when I first sent him the letter. What he said to me then was "That's my father you are saying that about. What does that say about me, his son?" An interesting response.

My mother's only comment was, "How could this have happened?"

I wonder, regularly, if they were surprised that I had forgotten. I wonder that now. I wonder how much they have forgotten, if anything.

What I know about my mother is that she was the youngest of three children. She wants life to be easy. She wants stuff – jewelry, collectibles, vacations, money, clothes.

She stayed home from work until my youngest sister went to first grade. Yet, I have no memory of her actually taking care of me. I remember being bathed by my older sister and babysat by my brother and home alone with my uncle and my older sister. I remember my mother reading romance novels and eating candy. She didn't like to cook.

And, recently, I remembered her at several cult rituals.

As all of this sinks in, my body releases the chemical addiction to my family of origin.

I had been considering sending a birthday card to my brother, but I've decided not to. The jury is still out on my brother. Although he's the only crumb left of any sort of kindness from that time, do I need that sort of crumb?

No, I do not.

Not now.

Right now, I need separation so that I can see all of it as real, heal, and then move on with my life and who I am.

Who I actually am. What do I like? What do I want? How do I have relationships with people? There are so many things I don't know. There is so much to process and realize and learn.

I read somewhere that the process of withdrawal from addiction, from beginning to end, can take up to two years before it's complete. That's a very long time. It's been about seven weeks so far since this physical withdrawal process began. It feels too long already.

Yet, after sixty years, well, a few more isn't really that much.

One more thing...

Before ending this book, I wanted to add one more piece to the story. I wanted to see if I had any access to myself as an older girl, but before all contact with the cult was stopped (by my decision to no longer participate).

A few months ago, I was able to reach my 3-year-old self, and know the decisions she made at that age. I was looking to add a bit more of my inner reasoning, at the end of all of this, to what seems impossible; blocking 14 years of horror that was my life. I wanted to get a sense of who I was.

I reached out today. Here is what happened.

I decided to reach for the age of 12. I have a photo of myself taken right before a St. Patrick's Day dance at the school I attended. A dance I was to perform in...

Me, age 12:

"I have to get ready for this stupid dance. I don't like doing it. Dancing. Not this dance. Not in this body. Nope. It's stupid."

"I thought it would be beautiful. It's stupid. These skirts are dumb. The dance is short. It is dumb. I feel silly doing it. Not beautiful."

Why are you doing it then?

"My teacher needed girls. A church thing. I'm Irish. I thought it would be cool. To do an Irish dance, an Irish jig. It never felt cool. It felt forced. Not pretty. Not cool. Dumb."

"Now I can't back out. Like everything else. I'm stuck. It's my job. It needs completing. Then at least it will be over."

What do you mean, "like everything else"?

"I have lots of jobs. Things that aren't beautiful that need completing. That have to get done. It's who I am. It's what I do."

I think you are very beautiful. The green skirt isn't perfect, but it's not bad. The group looks nice together, all the same.

"Yeah, well at least this job is in the light of day. I don't know if you are saying the truth. I can't see the group. I only know how I feel in this dumb, stiff, green skirt. I feel stupid."

Well, you don't look stupid.

Can you tell me about your other job? What it is and what it feels like?

"It's my family job. A secret family job I have to finish so we stay afloat. I have to go to these guys. The guys are creepy and crazy for something I don't understand."

"It is that way always."

"They seem regular when you see them on the street or <u>not</u> during my job – then the other times they go crazy."

"They are all the same, these men."

"They go crazy, hurt me while they lose their minds, and then push me away or to some other guy who wants that crazy thing."

"This is always my job."

"Some sort of crazy man thing."

"It keeps my family afloat."

"It hurts a lot. I don't complain. I'm not supposed to."

What about the robes?

The stuff in robes?

What happens then?

"HOW DO YOU KNOW ABOUT THAT!?"

I am you, just older.

"You cannot be me. I am."

Yes, but you live a long time. You also know things, see things, and leave your body. This lets you talk to me now. We are both safe. No one else knows.

"Well, I am not thinking this is right. This doesn't seem right. How could I talk to myself when I'm older? I'm not old now."

It is the same way you leave your body.

"I do that during my job."

I know that you do.

I will go then.

Maybe we'll talk again, if that's alright.

May I hug you?

"No. I don't like this. It feels weird."

Okay then. Goodbye.

So that was it.

Clearly, in the almost ten years between the first time I connected with her/me and this time, now age 12, she has learned a bit more.

She knows she is considered a financial necessity in the family.

She has learned on a deeper level, *not to trust what she does not fully comprehend,* even when it's me, even when it's herself.

She is clear on the danger of an outsider "knowing" about the cult. It explains a great deal, to me, about why I feel the way I do.

She still does not feel sorry for herself. She is something else again. A victim who somehow decided not to be.

Definitely angel material.

This is a True Story

Right before I was married to Fran, my father said something I didn't understand until now. I was in my wedding dress, he was in a tux, we'd just had photos taken. He said "Thank you for doing it my way."

Now I know what "his way" looks like. And so do you.

The Drawings

This is a True Story

RED ROBES open up the circle
& I go in middle
It feels like until 2
go with me — my uncle
& one Dr. RED ROBED
younger woman

But I can't really see
them once I'm in
there — I only see
me

"But I think" like this
Black robe. I
RED ROBES → with & young woman RED Robes
I almost want to poop
But White between them here mother father
that happens after.
I think
at some
point I
am alone in
in the circle of
Robes

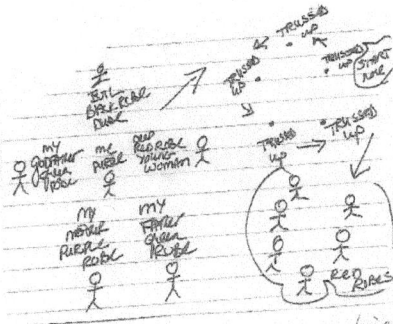

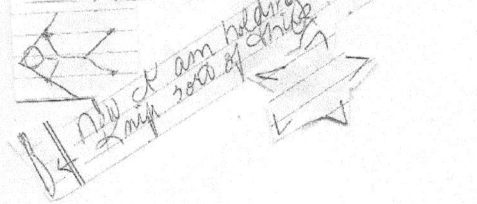

This is a True Story

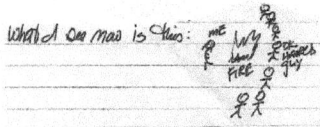

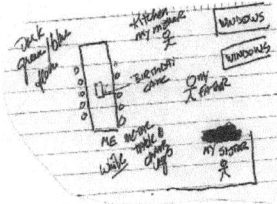

This is a True Story

Epilogue

Today it is exactly four months to the day since physical withdrawal began. Since that last recall, about five days ago, I've not had any further night wake ups and/or sweats. I've approached some sort of acceptance or realization or comprehension. It revolves around my uncle. My father. My family. My life. The puzzle pieces are fitting together.

It is such a bizarre idea to put into words, yet with that visual came a deep "grokking" of who my uncle is. He is a scumbag. Literally, figuratively and in every way imaginable. Until seeing that ritual, I'd completely obliterated the true evil predator that is my father's brother (not to mention my father and my mother) from my memory.

I now know why I chose to split my memory/mind. The reality of it would have shattered the possibility of having anything close to a "normal" life, let alone a happy ending.

Instead, I've known love. I've raised four sensitive, remarkable and beautiful children. I've been blessed with marriages to two fine men who love their families. I have some very dear, and very close friends. I have work that fulfills me and helps others. I am extremely grateful for these things.

All of that happened. In the same lifetime you've just finished reading about. The hideous abuse that was my first fourteen years is over. It stopped in the early 1970's.

It stopped because at the age of fourteen I was given a choice.

I chose NO.

I did not continue to participate.

I neatly and completely hid any evidence that it was real at all. I hid it from myself, splitting my mind in order to keep it hidden.

I kept it from everyone I knew.

Emotionally, I have gaps. They are empty places that should be filled up with things like infant/parent bonding. Things like trust. I never knew safety or protection from harm.

I knew life only as a series of events, most of them terrifying and painful, in which I had to perform something. If I did not, I would die. Or perhaps, someone close to me would suffer. I did not want to die, so I performed. I performed whatever I had to. I did this because I wanted to live, as insane as that may seem now that the truth of my life is out in the open. I did what I was told, from some internal will to survive.

I cannot excuse myself from participating in any of what I've recalled. I see, feel, hear, smell and taste the complete horror that was my first fourteen years. These memories are no longer hidden. I have accessed the awful and I am still standing.

Part of the reason may be so that this story gets told. In this "me too" era of pedophile exposure, mine is clearly not the only childhood like this. Perhaps now others will come forward.

If you are reading this, and you too hold a similarly unbelievable and terrible secret, I encourage you to do so. Come out safely and anonymously. Until the dark underbelly of our sadistic obsessions is brought to light, it will not be stopped.

As the fact of these memories takes hold, there is a temptation to stumble once more into forgetting. It would seem the easier choice. They are scenes from a horror movie. Yet I've done that already.

I am here now, speaking to you, because a part of me chose to be. I lived. My choice now, rather than to for-get, is to for-give. Forgive myself for all that I have done and not done. This will take the rest of my life.

I will tell you that when the headline news tells you of people who shoot up restaurants, schools or movie theaters, and when asked later, have no recall of having done so, that it is possible. There are very sophisticated drugs, and programming/brainwashing techniques that create it as a possibility. I know. I lived for 14 years, swimming in a sea of both drugs and brainwashing, and did not remember it completely <u>for another 45 years</u>. It took a near fatal car accident to jar me awake.

It also must be said here that once programmed, *the compelling theater of satanic abuse ritual creates for the victim an iron clad reason to keep quiet* (if you do, in fact, remember). There are witnesses to your participation. You've done the unthinkable.

This story sounds unbelievable. This story is true.

It didn't happen in Hollywood or Washington DC or on some rich man's island.

It happened in a small coastal town; in the town hall, at the fire station, in various homes and on beautiful beaches. It happened in barns. It happened on farmer's fields. It happened in liquor stores. It happened in parking lots. It happened in living rooms.

The men and women weren't actors or elite. They were doctors, teachers, housewives, students, servicemen, principals, farmers, local politicians, fishermen, secretaries, merchants, morticians, indigents, children, teenagers, fraternity boys. Townspeople. Average Americans.

Before I could walk, I was witness to a killing. At the age of two, my father performed oral sex on me in his lazy-boy, my uncle molested me, as did many other men; men in suits.

From then on, I was regularly delivered to an assortment of men for sex. Some of this was during satanic rituals. Some of this was a sort of side business of my parents. My uncle drove me places. My father drove me places. I was pimped out by my older sister to her friends; by my mother. Sometimes I rode my bike to places I was told to go.

The various rituals at times included capes, at other times, costumes. Once there was a wolf costume. I was dressed as Little Red Riding Hood. Once there was a prince. I was a princess in a blue taffeta gown.

Most of the details are in the story you've just read. What I want to leave you with is this...

I have not given the actual names of people or places because this is not a fairy tale. This is real. People are killed when there is a threat of exposure. I got the message. Absolutely and clearly.

Right now, there is a child being molested, tortured or killed in your town. Right now. Day or night, it matters not. I escaped. I'm one of the fortunate ones.

A portion of the royalties from the sale of this book goes to child rescue organizations. Your purchase helps support these brave men and women who are shining a light on this unfathomable darkness hiding in our culture.

Thank you.

The trailer park angel

9.28.19

This is a True Story

The end

www.ingramcontent.com/pod-product-compliance
Lightning Source LLC
Chambersburg PA
CBHW021500090426
42739CB00007B/403